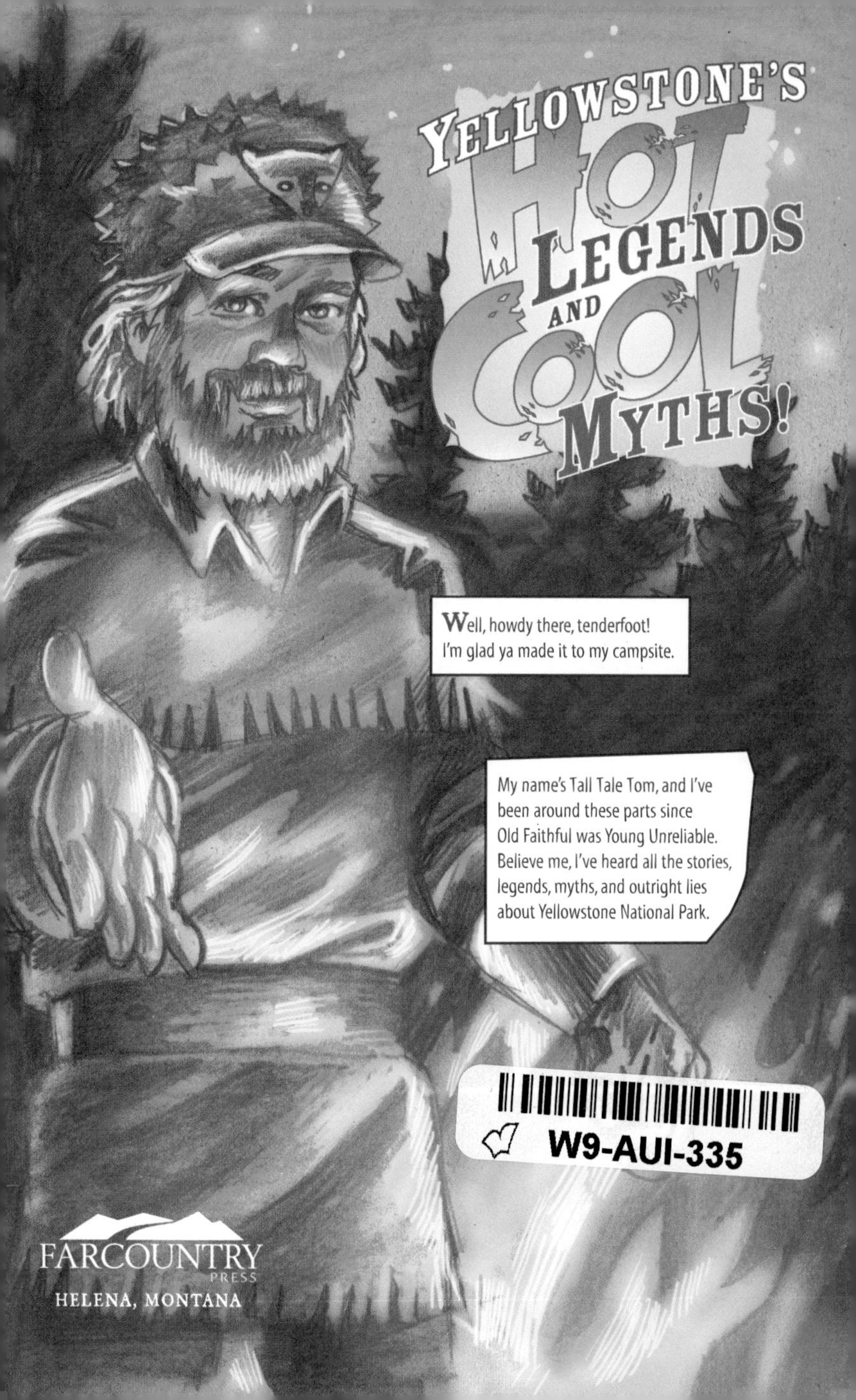
YELLOWSTONE'S
HOT LEGENDS AND COOL MYTHS!
Well, howdy there, tenderfoot! I'm glad ya made it to my campsite.
My name's Tall Tale Tom, and I've been around these parts since Old Faithful was Young Unreliable. Believe me, I've heard all the stories, legends, myths, and outright lies about Yellowstone National Park.

FARCOUNTRY PRESS
HELENA, MONTANA

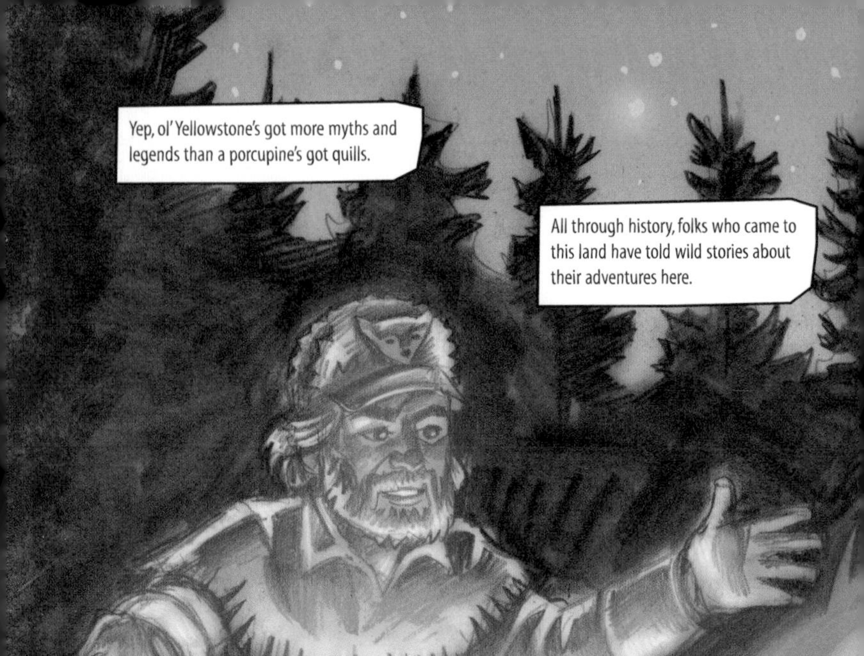
Yep, ol' Yellowstone's got more myths and legends than a porcupine's got quills.
All through history, folks who came to this land have told wild stories about their adventures here.

ISBN 10: 1-56037-485-3
ISBN 13: 978-1-56037-485-5

For more information on our books, write Farcountry Press, P.O. Box 5630, Helena, MT 59604; call (800) 821-3874; or visit www.farcountrypress.com.

Created, produced, and designed in the United States.
Printed in China.

15 14 13 12 11 10 09 1 2 3 4 5 6 7

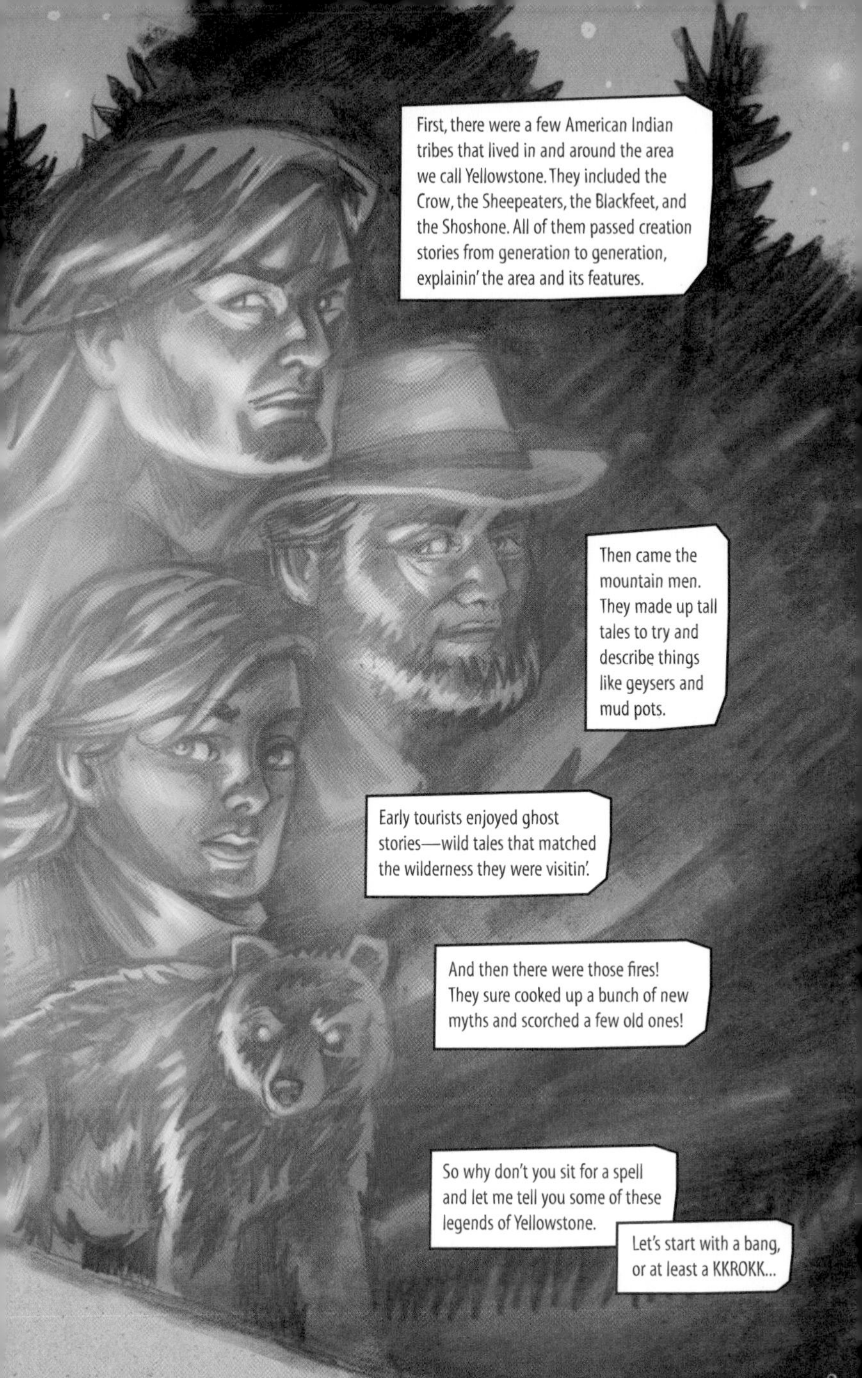
First, there were a few American Indian tribes that lived in and around the area we call Yellowstone. They included the Crow, the Sheepeaters, the Blackfeet, and the Shoshone. All of them passed creation stories from generation to generation, explainin' the area and its features.
Then came the mountain men. They made up tall tales to try and describe things like geysers and mud pots.
Early tourists enjoyed ghost stories—wild tales that matched the wilderness they were visitin'.
And then there were those fires! They sure cooked up a bunch of new myths and scorched a few old ones!
So why don't you sit for a spell and let me tell you some of these legends of Yellowstone.
Let's start with a bang, or at least a KKROKK...

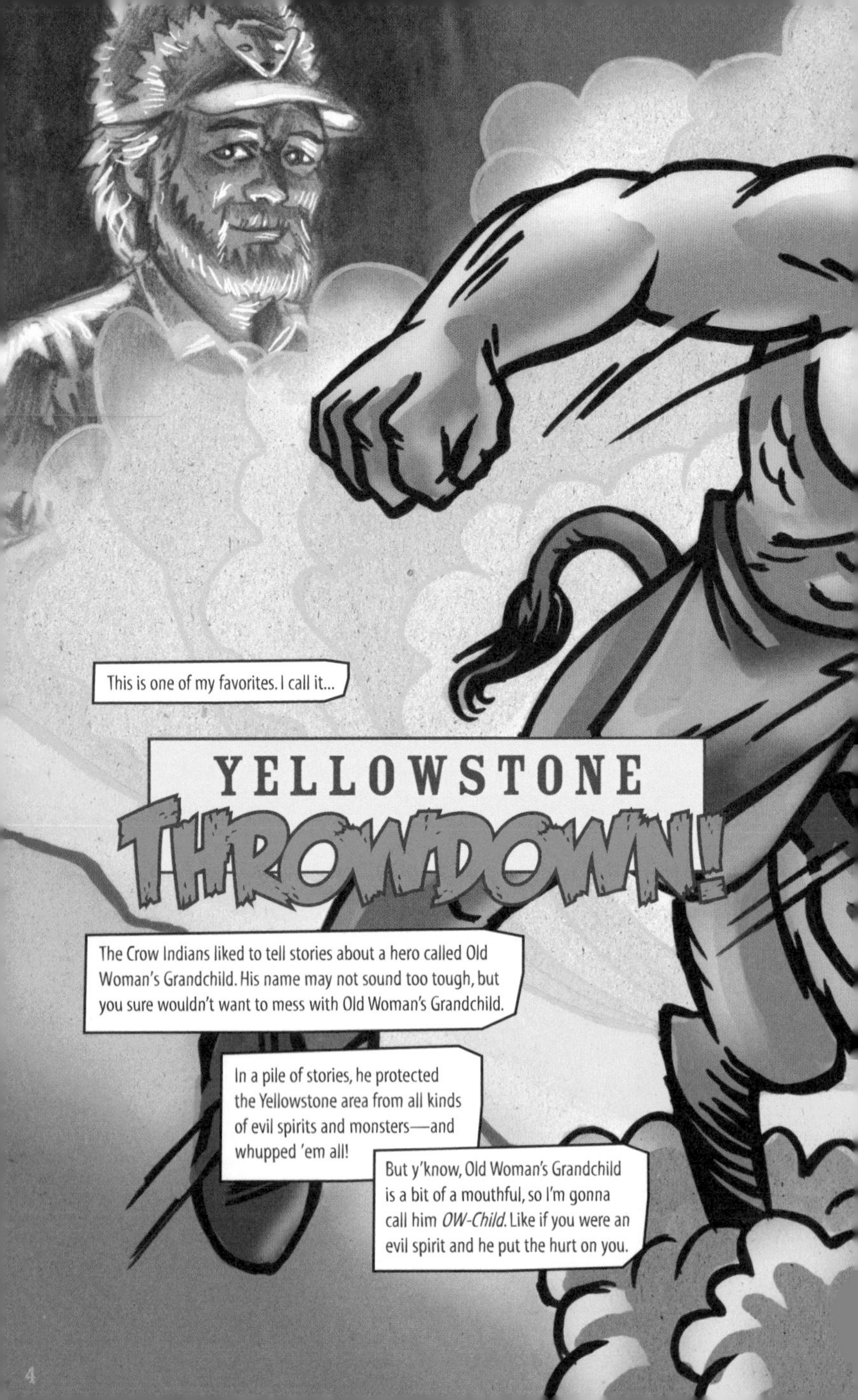
This is one of my favorites. I call it...
YELLOWSTONE
THROWDOWN!
The Crow Indians liked to tell stories about a hero called Old Woman's Grandchild. His name may not sound too tough, but you sure wouldn't want to mess with Old Woman's Grandchild.
In a pile of stories, he protected the Yellowstone area from all kinds of evil spirits and monsters—and whupped 'em all!
But y'know, Old Woman's Grandchild is a bit of a mouthful, so I'm gonna call him *OW-Child*. Like if you were an evil spirit and he put the hurt on you.

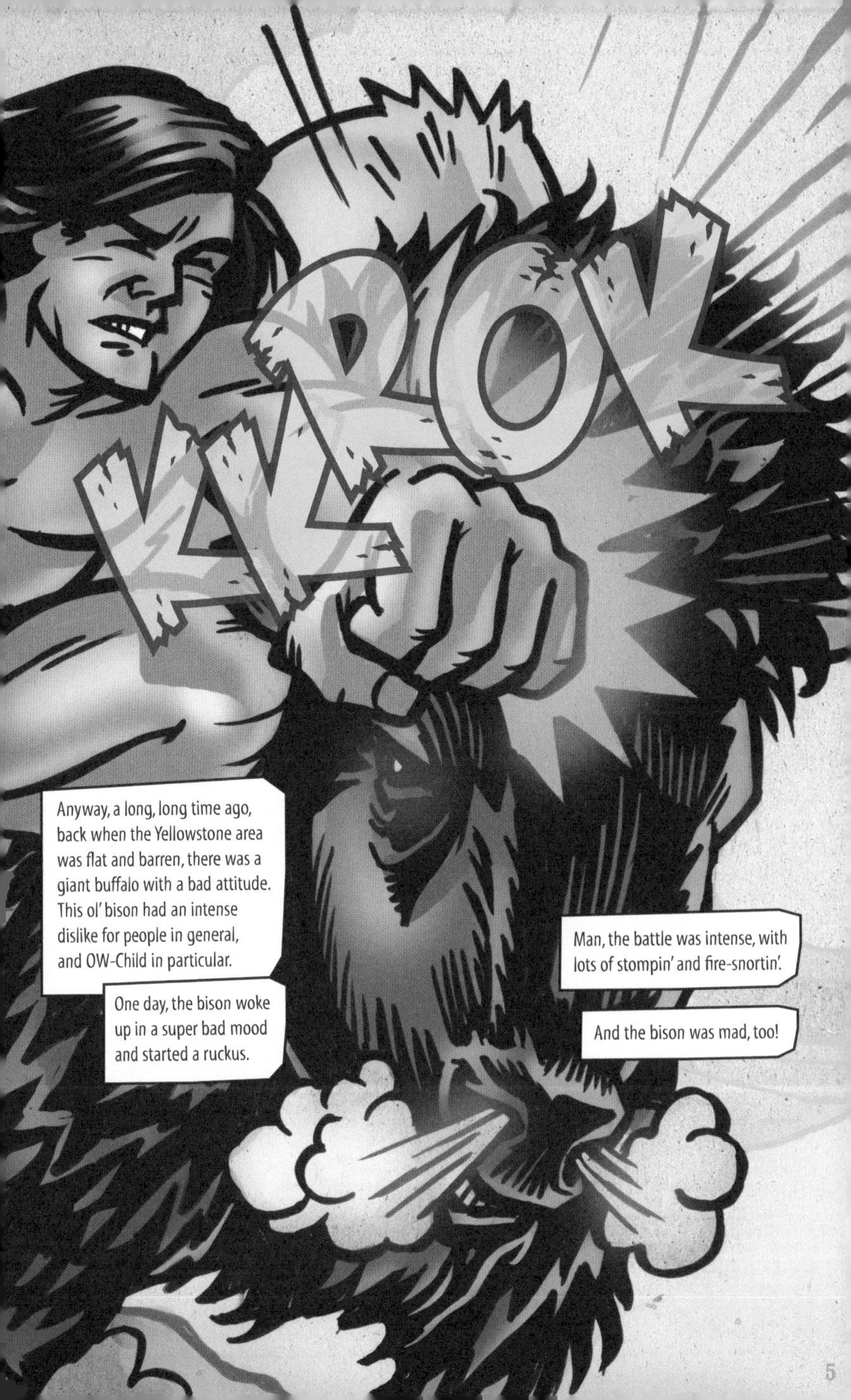
KAPOW
Anyway, a long, long time ago, back when the Yellowstone area was flat and barren, there was a giant buffalo with a bad attitude. This ol' bison had an intense dislike for people in general, and OW-Child in particular.
One day, the bison woke up in a super bad mood and started a ruckus.
Man, the battle was intense, with lots of stompin' and fire-snortin'.
And the bison was mad, too!

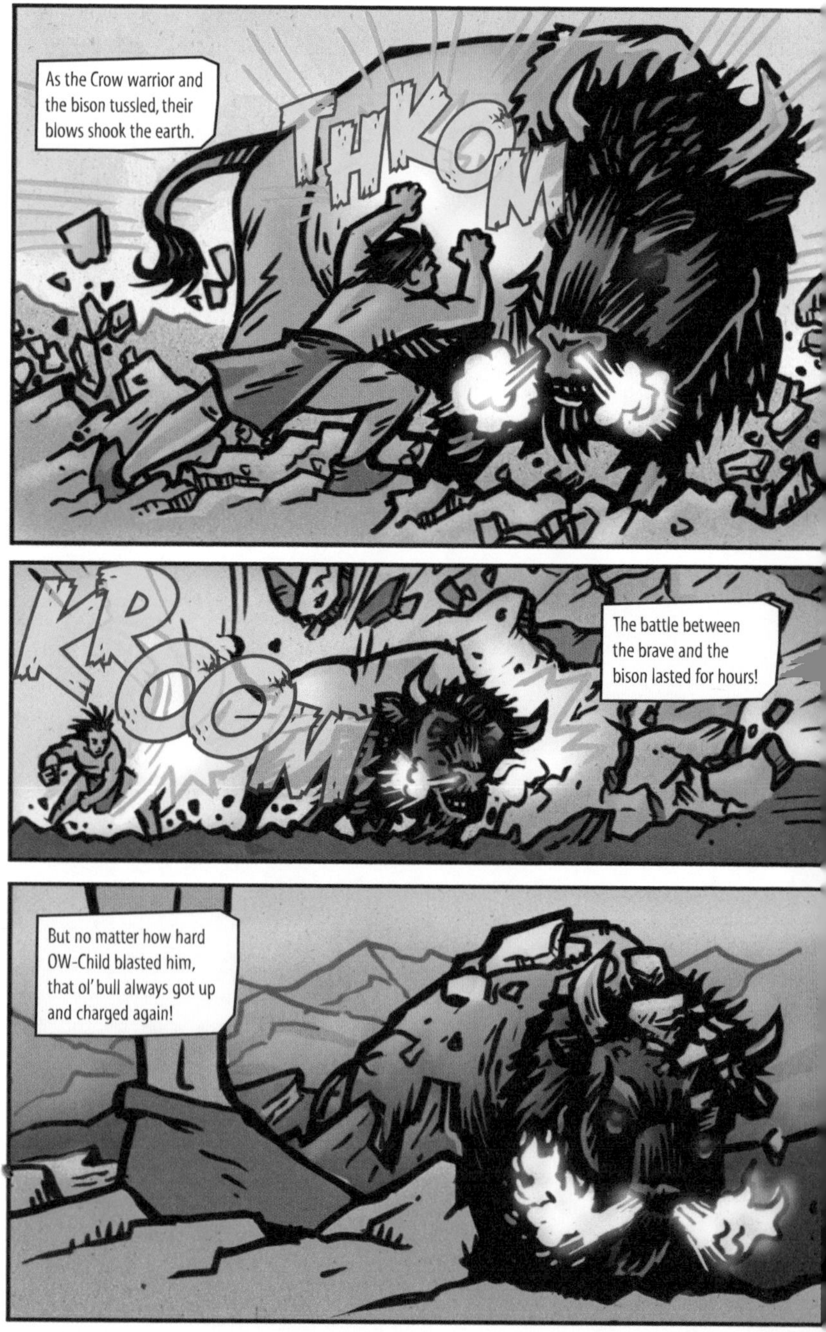
As the Crow warrior and the bison tussled, their blows shook the earth.
THKOOM
KROOM
The battle between the brave and the bison lasted for hours!
But no matter how hard OW-Child blasted him, that ol' bull always got up and charged again!

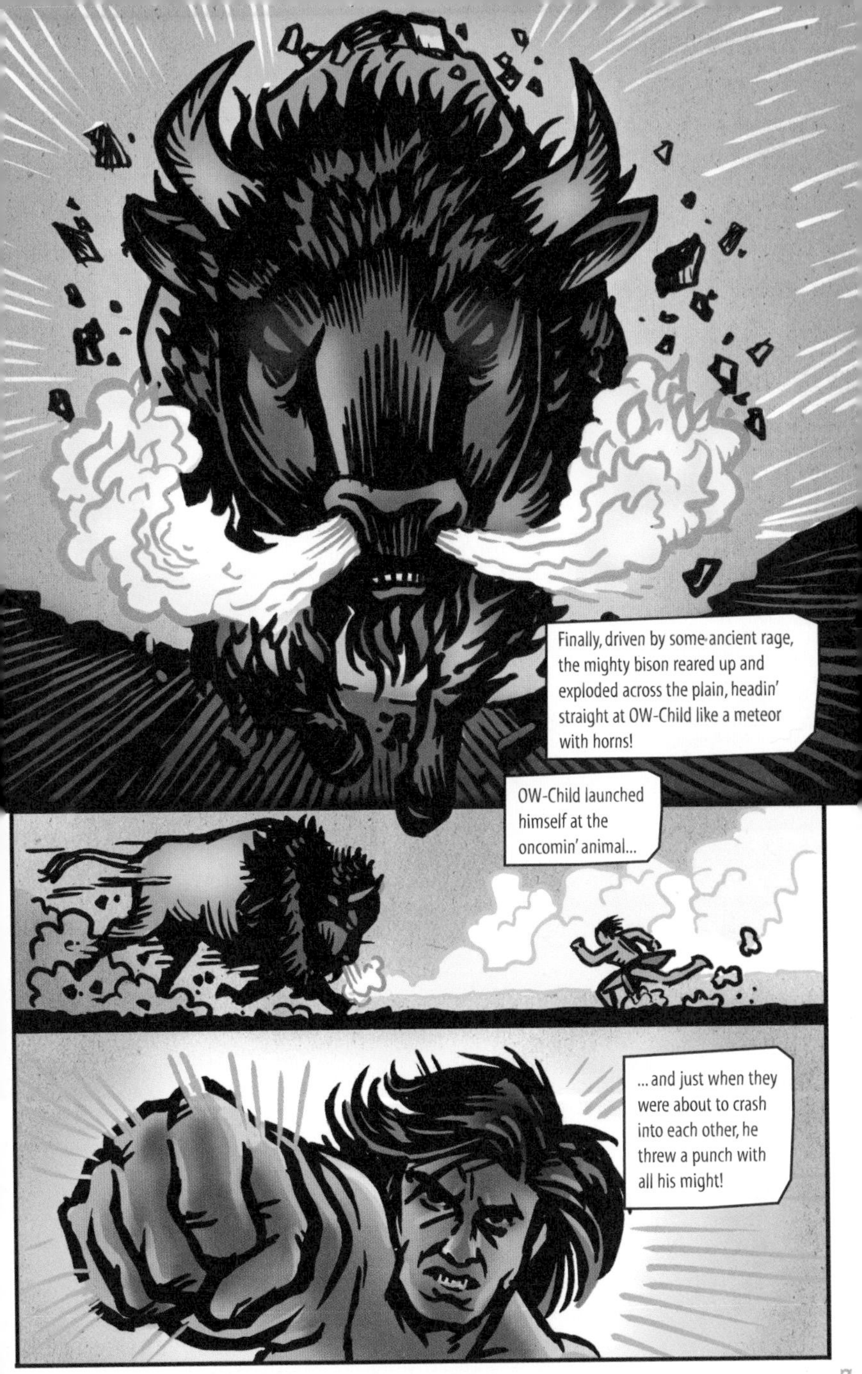
Finally, driven by some ancient rage, the mighty bison reared up and exploded across the plain, headin' straight at OW-Child like a meteor with horns!
OW-Child launched himself at the oncomin' animal...
... and just when they were about to crash into each other, he threw a punch with all his might!

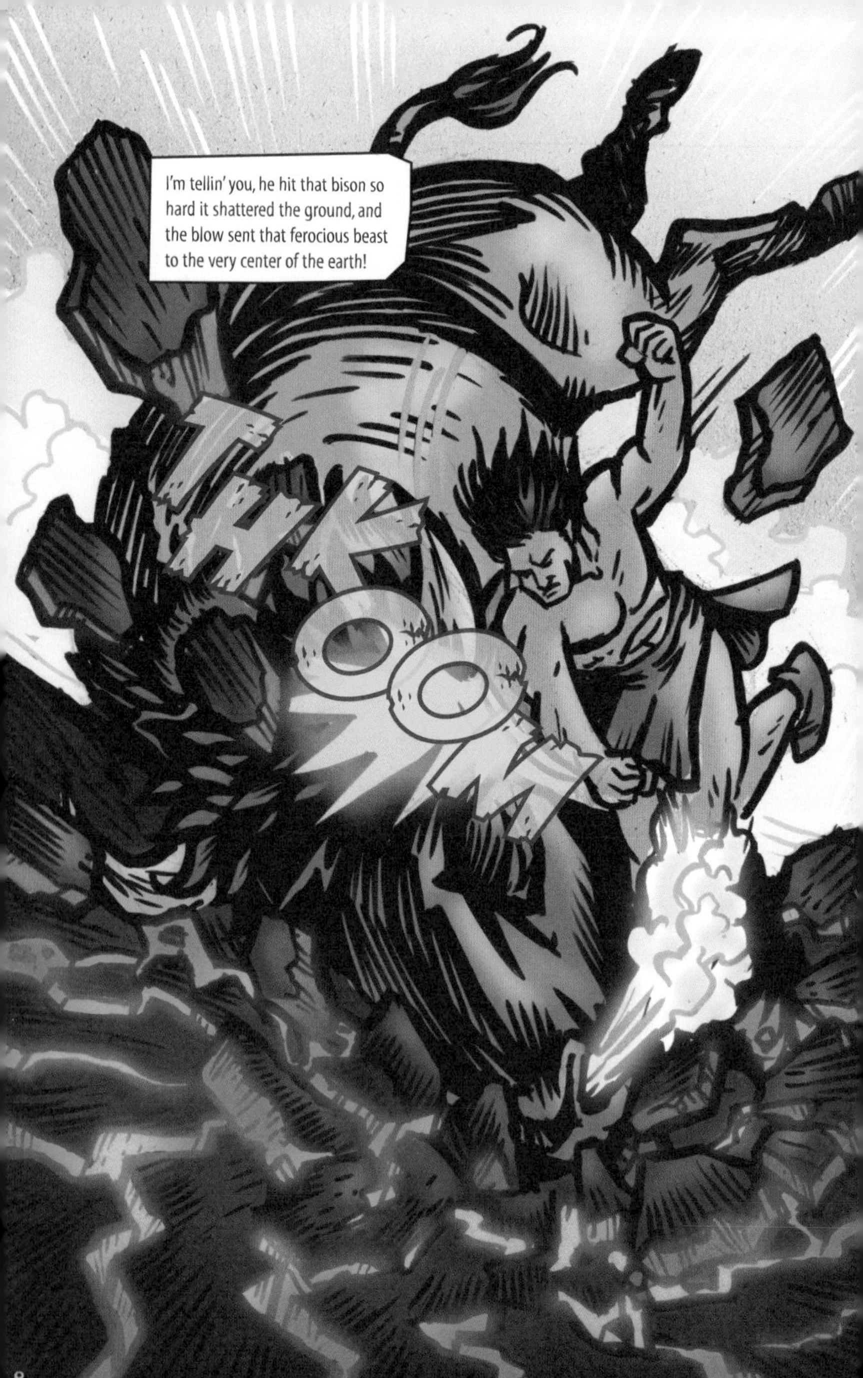
I'm tellin' you, he hit that bison so hard it shattered the ground, and the blow sent that ferocious beast to the very center of the earth!
THKOOM

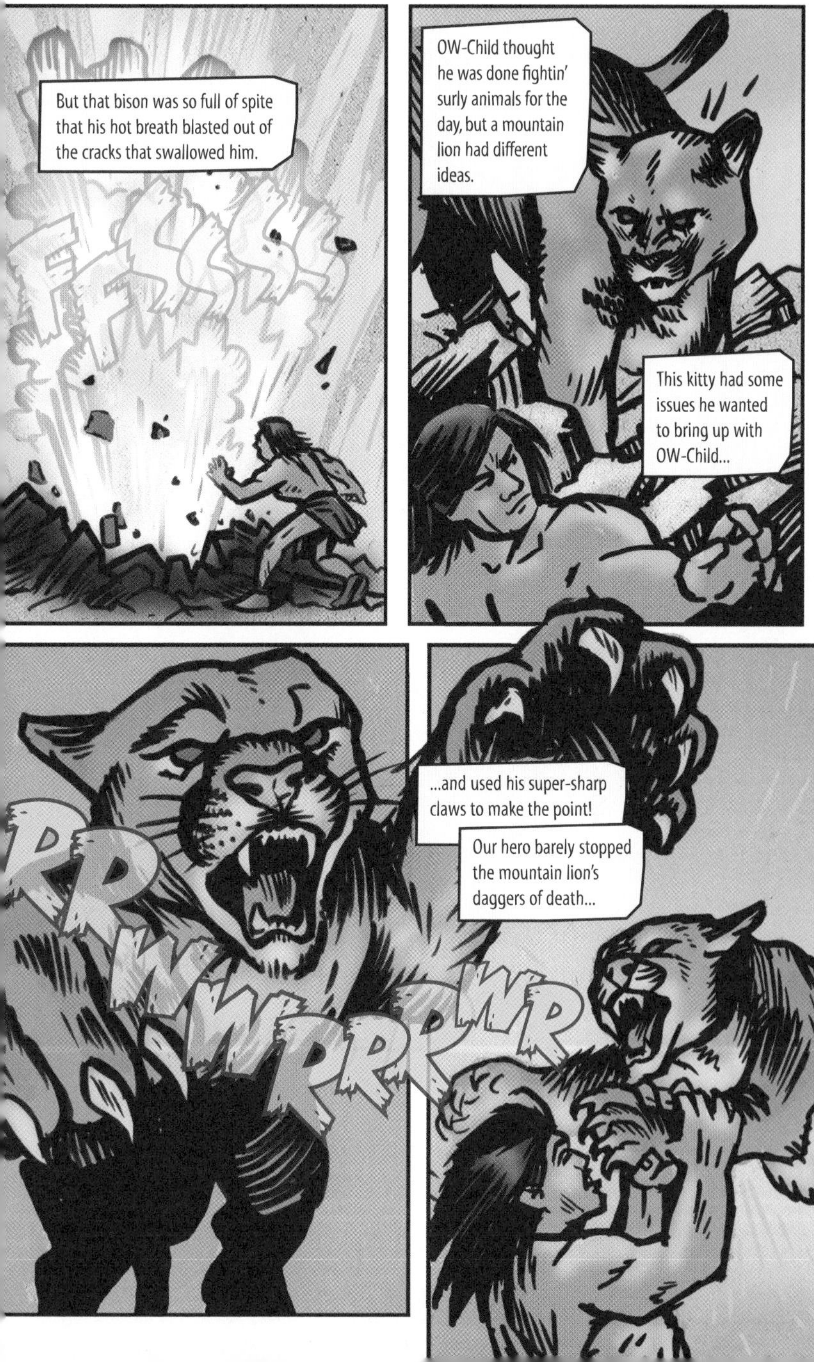
But that bison was so full of spite that his hot breath blasted out of the cracks that swallowed him.
OW-Child thought he was done fightin' surly animals for the day, but a mountain lion had different ideas.
This kitty had some issues he wanted to bring up with OW-Child...
...and used his super-sharp claws to make the point!
Our hero barely stopped the mountain lion's daggers of death...

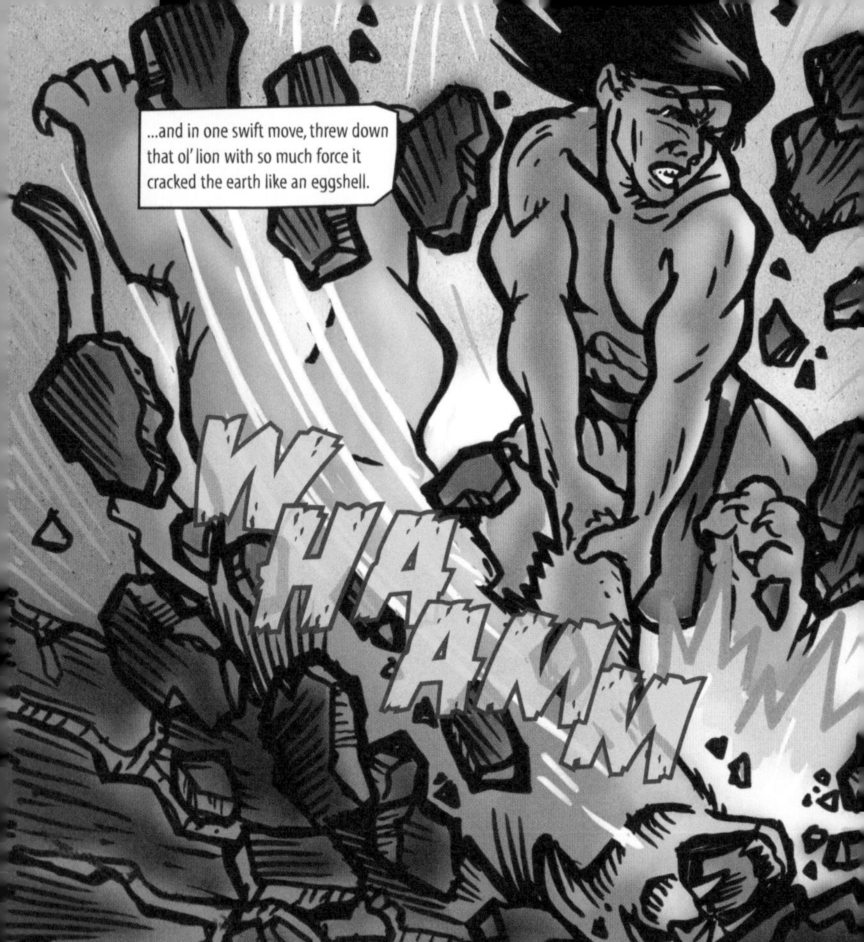
...and in one swift move, threw down that ol' lion with so much force it cracked the earth like an eggshell.
WHAAMM

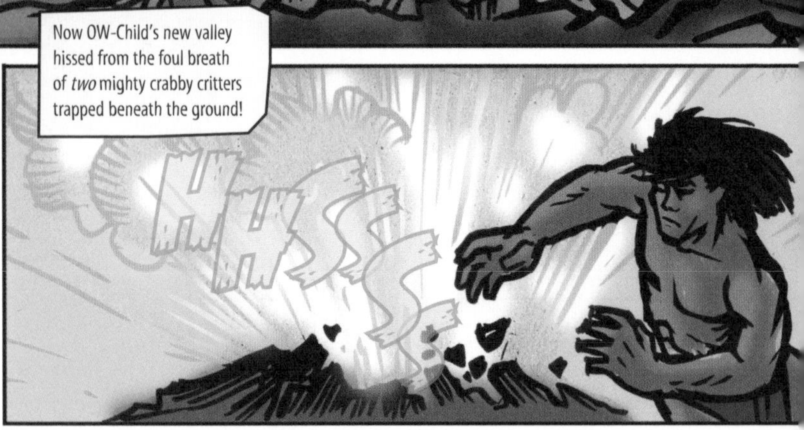
Now OW-Child's new valley hissed from the foul breath of *two* mighty crabby critters trapped beneath the ground!
HHSSS

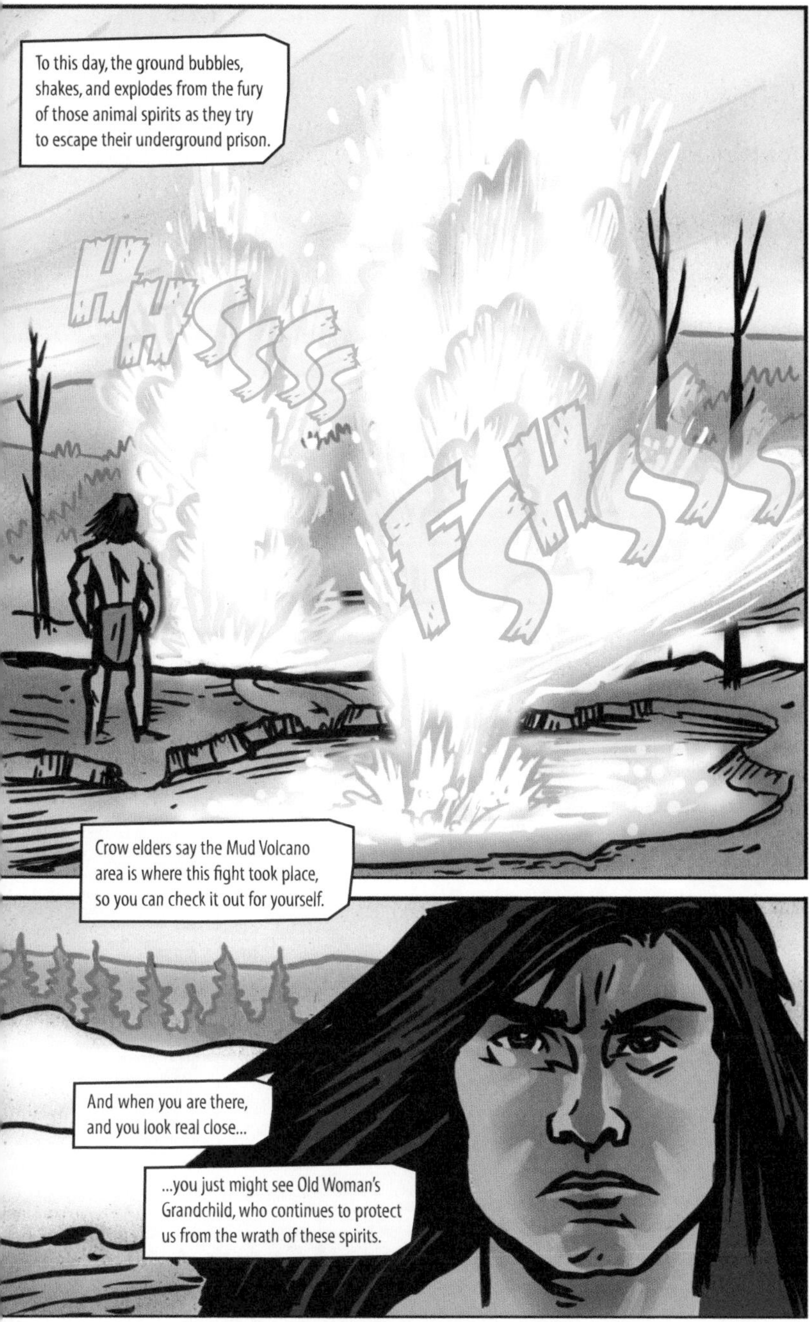
To this day, the ground bubbles, shakes, and explodes from the fury of those animal spirits as they try to escape their underground prison.
HHSSS
FSHSSS
Crow elders say the Mud Volcano area is where this fight took place, so you can check it out for yourself.
And when you are there, and you look real close...
...you just might see Old Woman's Grandchild, who continues to protect us from the wrath of these spirits.

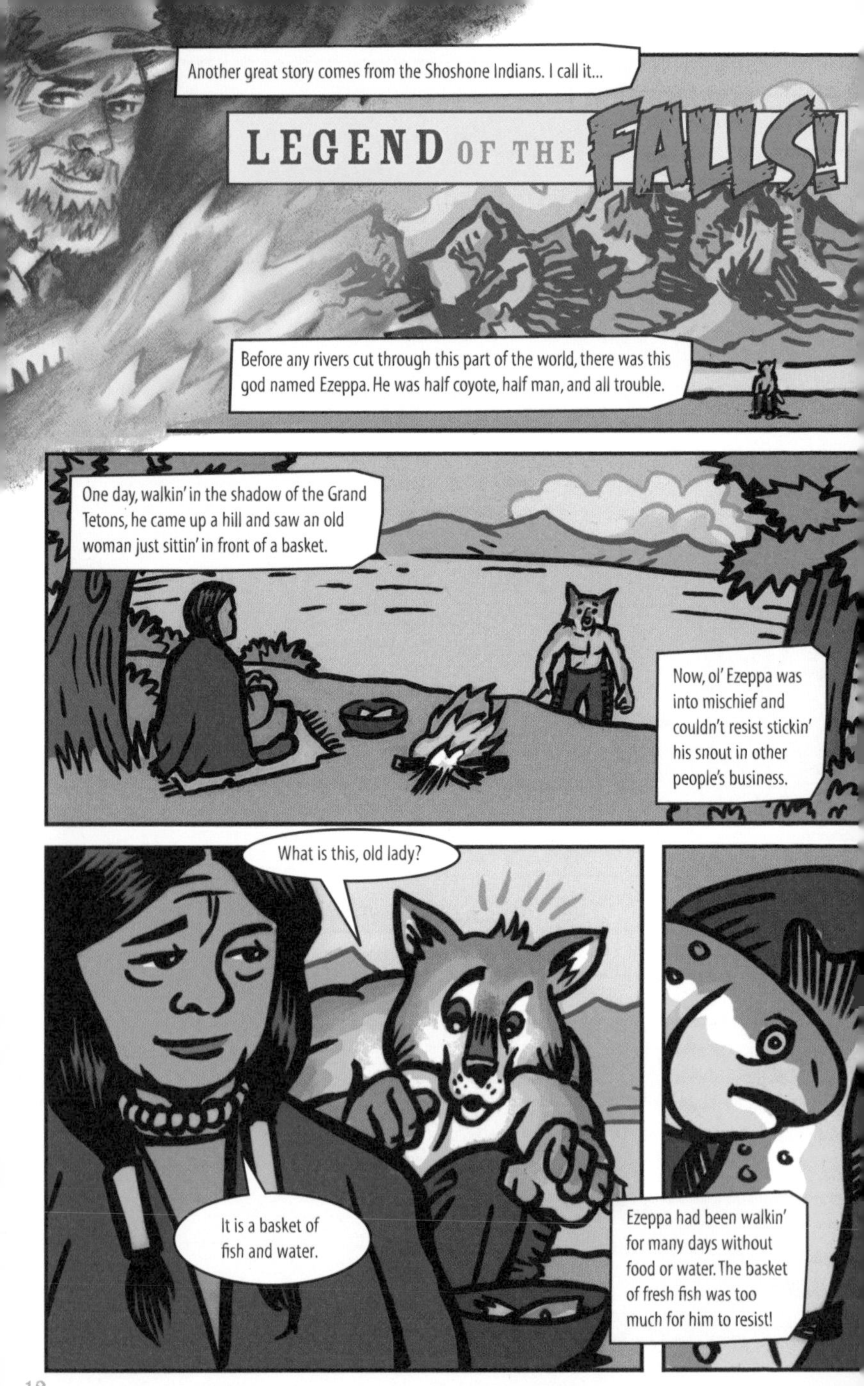

Another great story comes from the Shoshone Indians. I call it...
LEGEND OF THE FALLS!
Before any rivers cut through this part of the world, there was this god named Ezeppa. He was half coyote, half man, and all trouble.
One day, walkin' in the shadow of the Grand Tetons, he came up a hill and saw an old woman just sittin' in front of a basket.
Now, ol' Ezeppa was into mischief and couldn't resist stickin' his snout in other people's business.
What is this, old lady?
It is a basket of fish and water.
Ezeppa had been walkin' for many days without food or water. The basket of fresh fish was too much for him to resist!

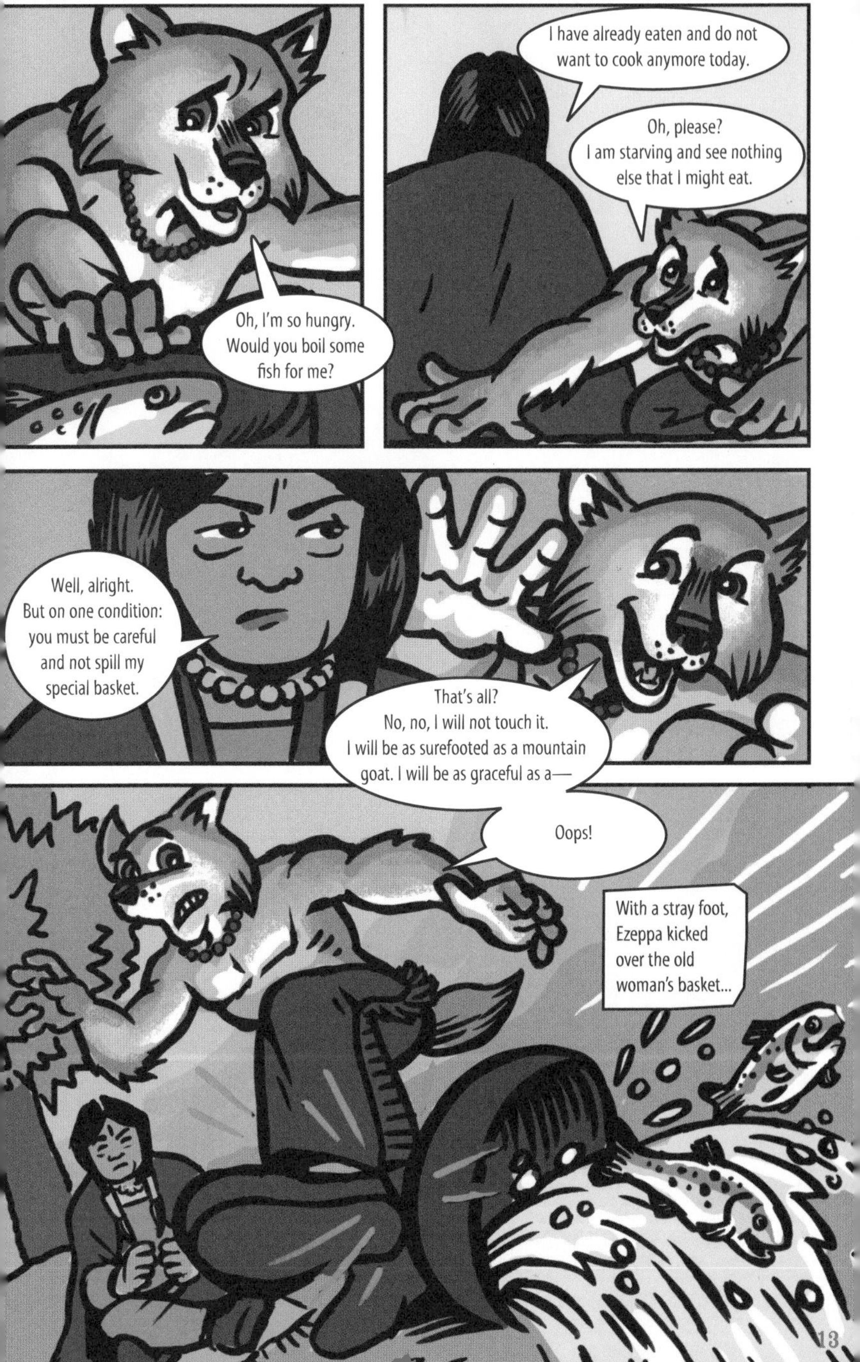
Oh, I'm so hungry. Would you boil some fish for me?
I have already eaten and do not want to cook anymore today.
Oh, please? I am starving and see nothing else that I might eat.
Well, alright. But on one condition: you must be careful and not spill my special basket.
That's all? No, no, I will not touch it. I will be as surefooted as a mountain goat. I will be as graceful as a—
Oops!
With a stray foot, Ezeppa kicked over the old woman's basket...

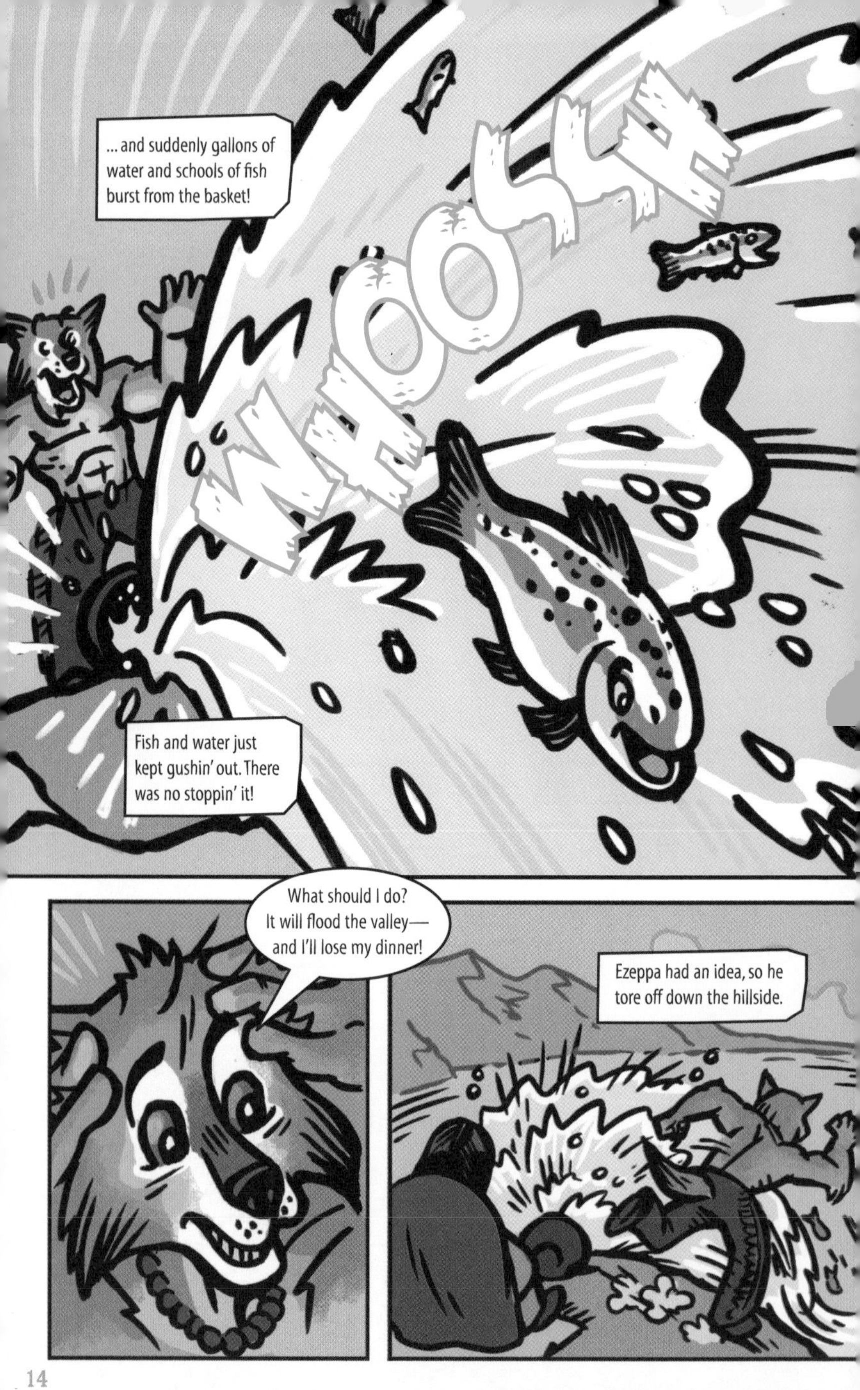
... and suddenly gallons of water and schools of fish burst from the basket!
WHOOSH
Fish and water just kept gushin' out. There was no stoppin' it!
What should I do? It will flood the valley—and I'll lose my dinner!
Ezeppa had an idea, so he tore off down the hillside.

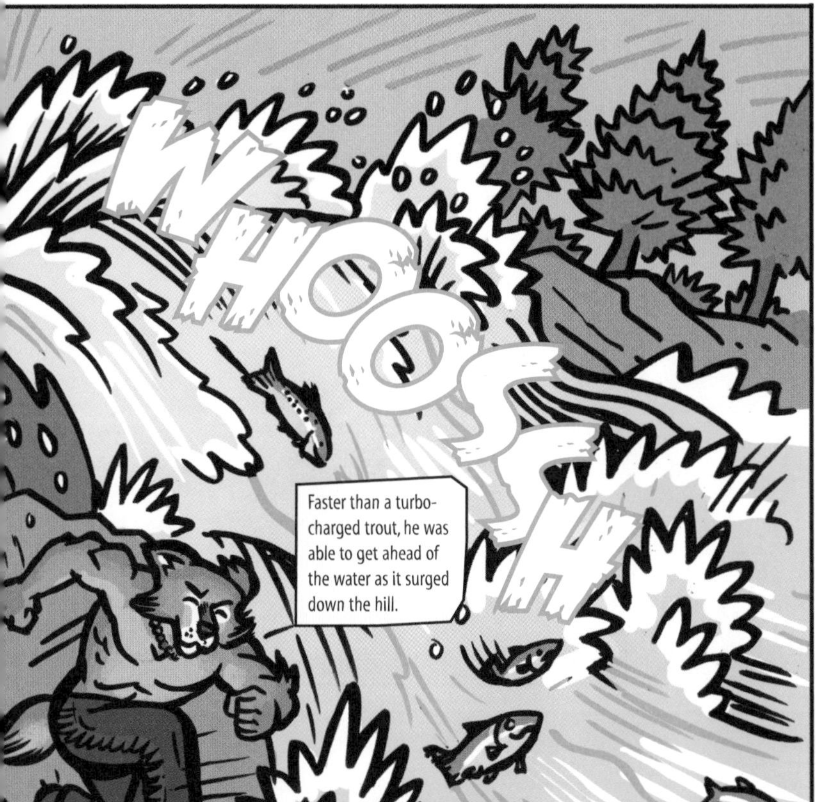
WHOOSH
Faster than a turbo-charged trout, he was able to get ahead of the water as it surged down the hill.

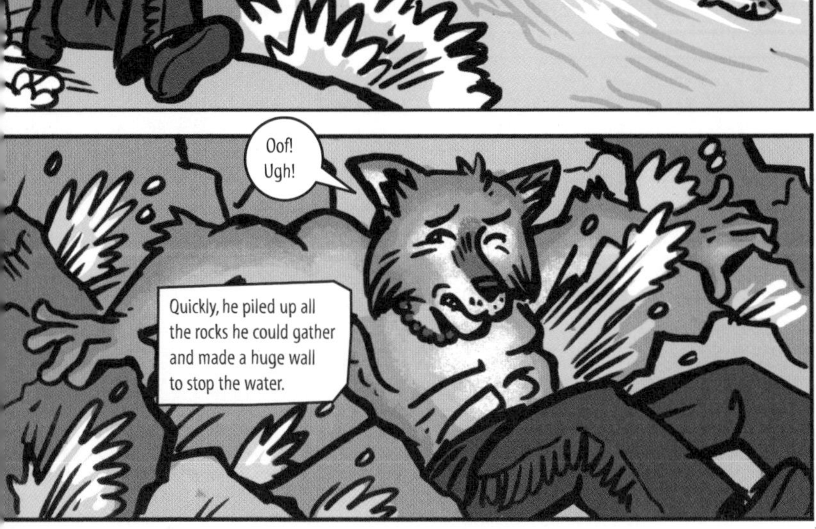
Oof! Ugh!
Quickly, he piled up all the rocks he could gather and made a huge wall to stop the water.

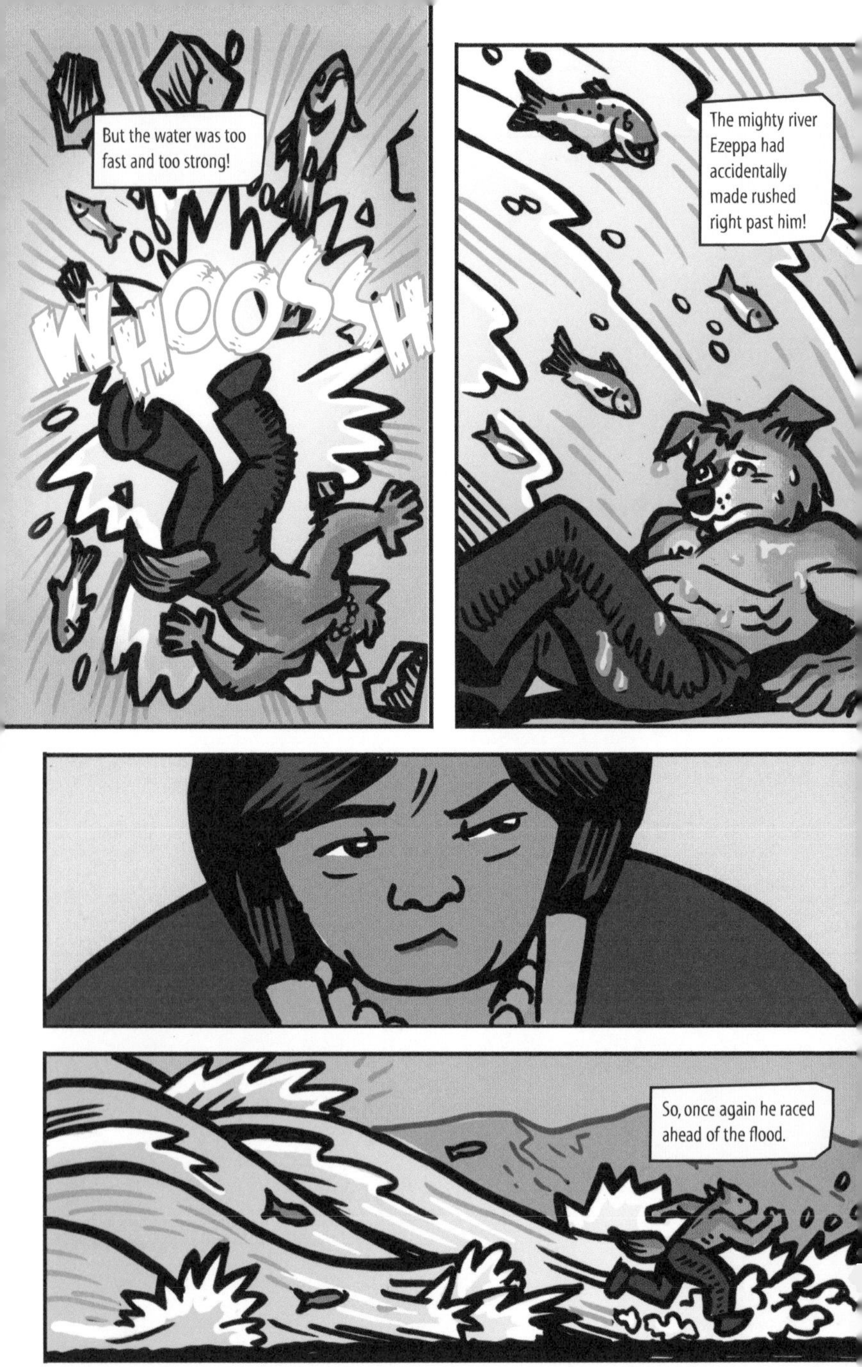
But the water was too fast and too strong!
WHOOSSH
The mighty river Ezeppa had accidentally made rushed right past him!
So, once again he raced ahead of the flood.

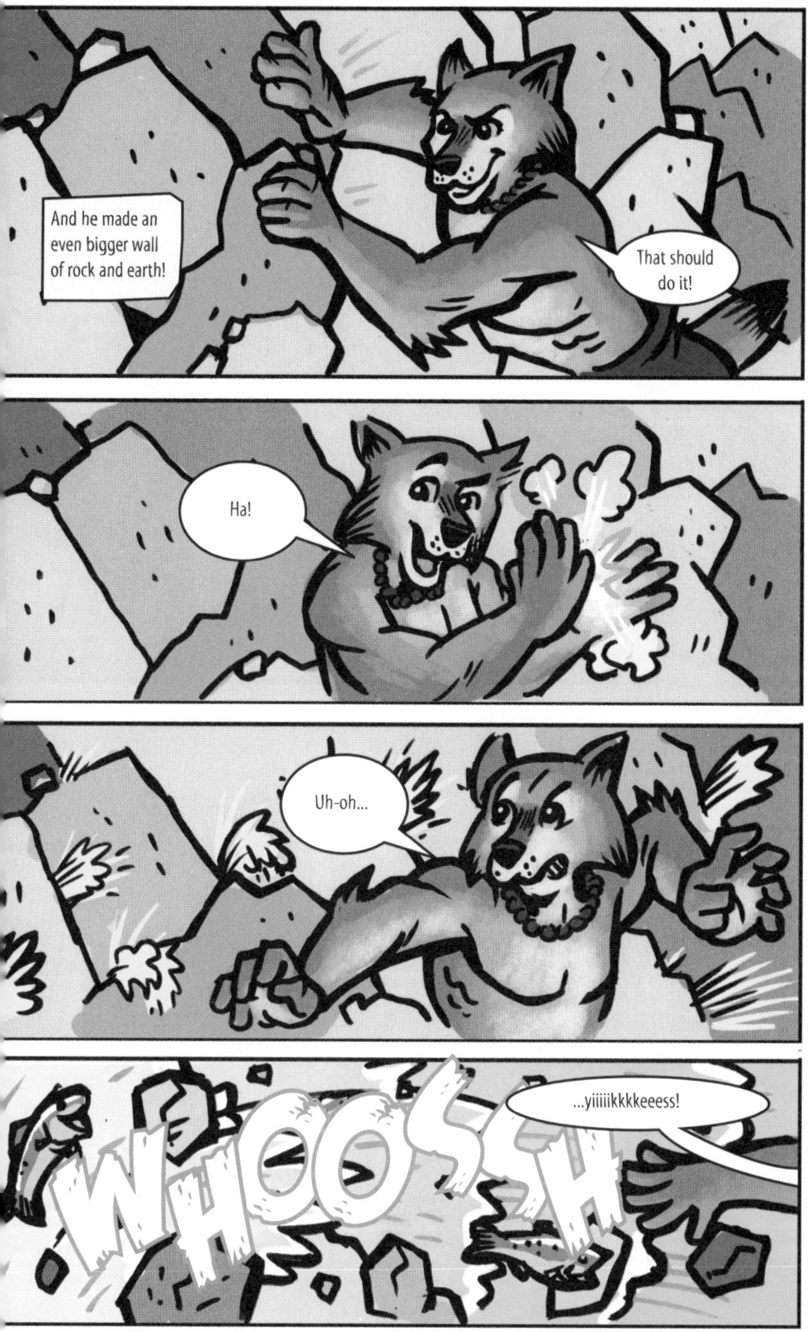
And he made an even bigger wall of rock and earth!
That should do it!
Ha!
Uh-oh...
WHOOSH
...yiiiiikkkkeeess!

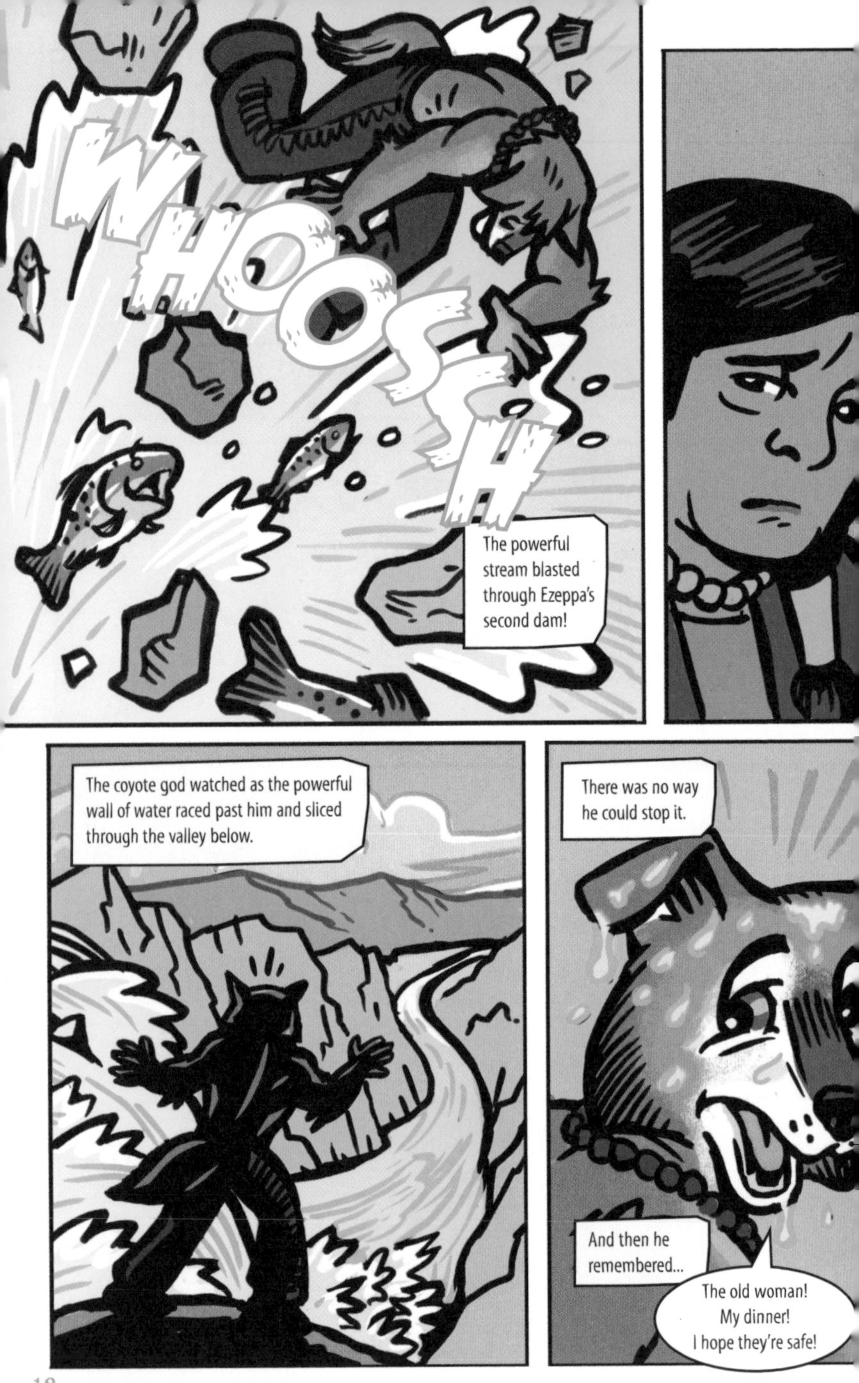

WHOOSCH
The powerful stream blasted through Ezeppa's second dam!
The coyote god watched as the powerful wall of water raced past him and sliced through the valley below.
There was no way he could stop it.
And then he remembered...
The old woman! My dinner! I hope they're safe!

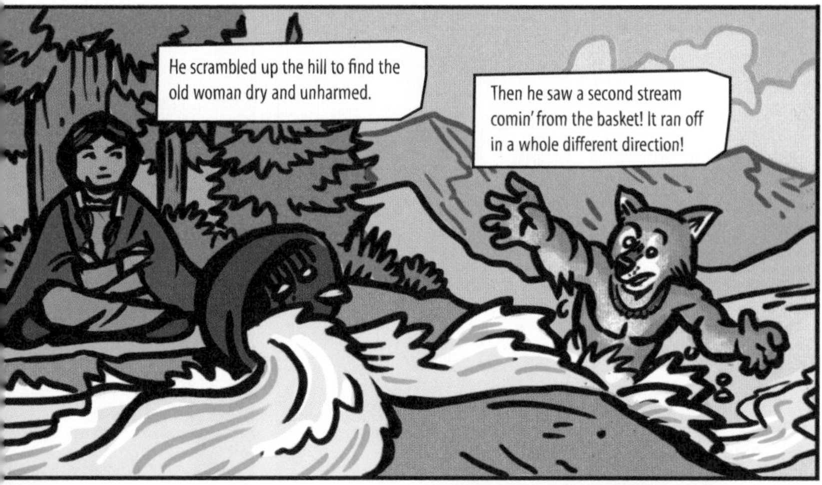
He scrambled up the hill to find the old woman dry and unharmed.
Then he saw a second stream comin' from the basket! It ran off in a whole different direction!

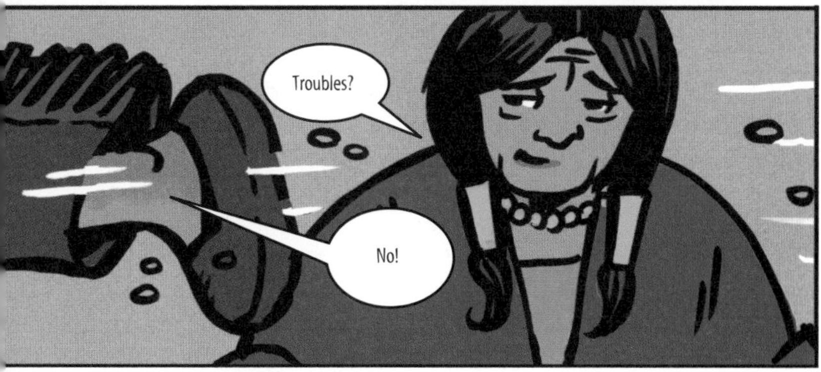
Troubles?
No!

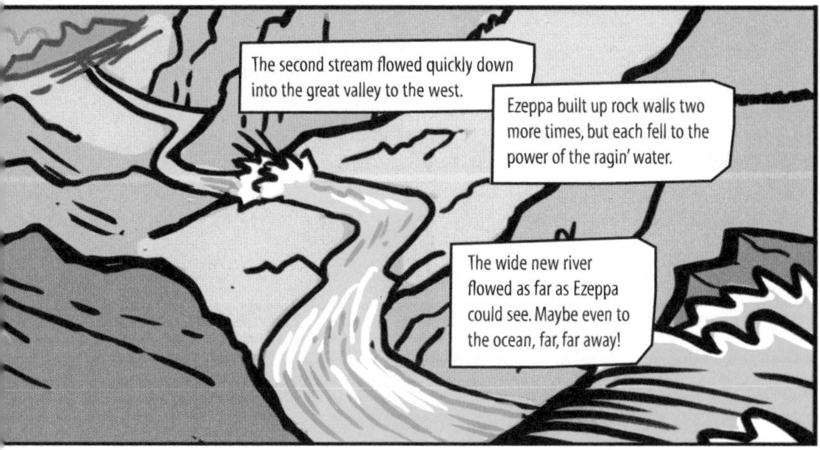
The second stream flowed quickly down into the great valley to the west.
Ezeppa built up rock walls two more times, but each fell to the power of the ragin' water.
The wide new river flowed as far as Ezeppa could see. Maybe even to the ocean, far, far away!

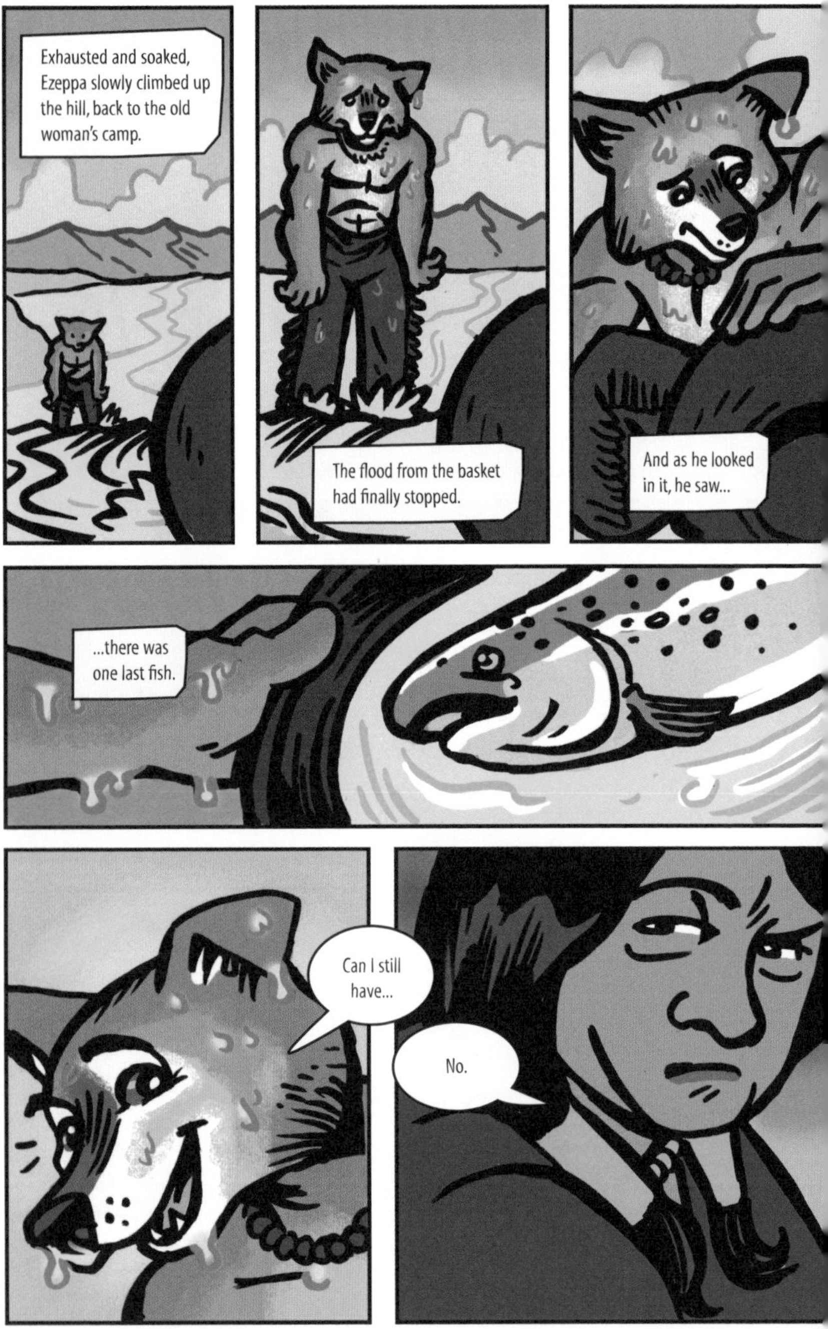
Exhausted and soaked, Ezeppa slowly climbed up the hill, back to the old woman's camp.
The flood from the basket had finally stopped.
And as he looked in it, he saw...
...there was one last fish.
Can I still have...
No.

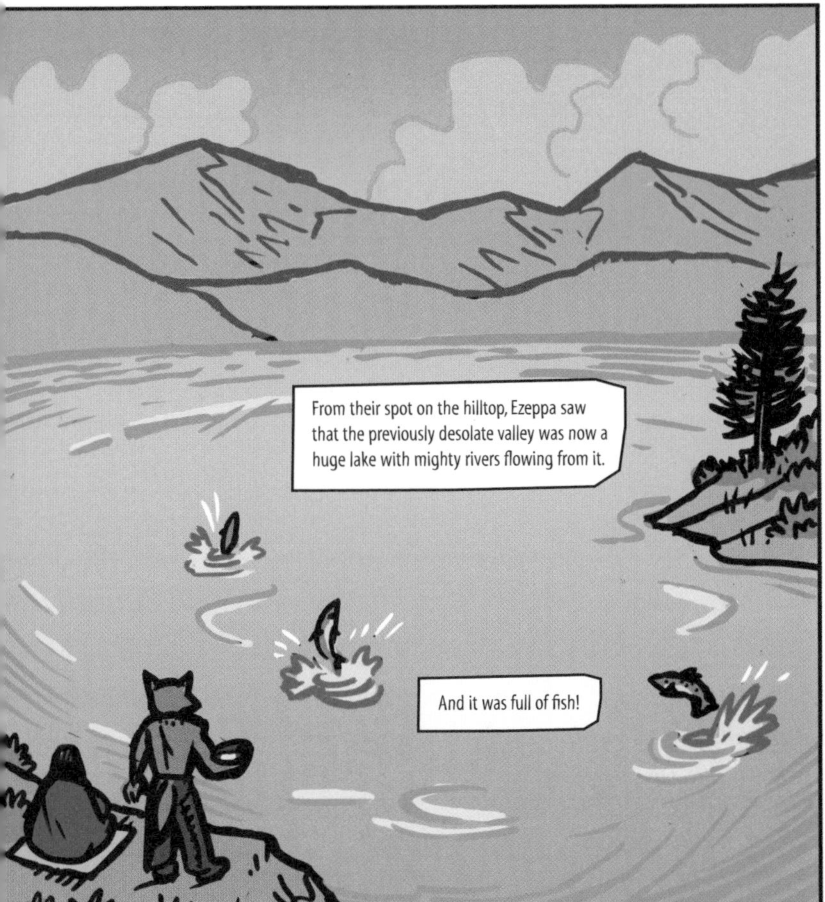
From their spot on the hilltop, Ezeppa saw that the previously desolate valley was now a huge lake with mighty rivers flowing from it.
And it was full of fish!

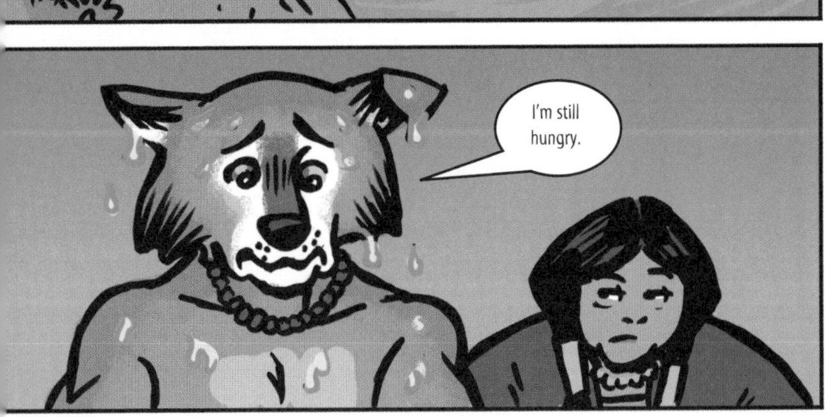
I'm still hungry.

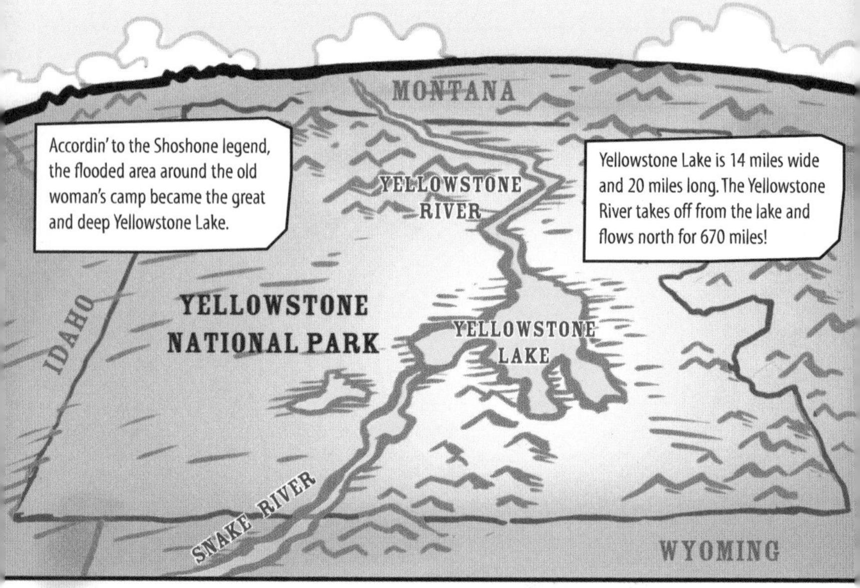
Accordin' to the Shoshone legend, the flooded area around the old woman's camp became the great and deep Yellowstone Lake.
MONTANA
YELLOWSTONE RIVER
Yellowstone Lake is 14 miles wide and 20 miles long. The Yellowstone River takes off from the lake and flows north for 670 miles!
IDAHO
YELLOWSTONE NATIONAL PARK
YELLOWSTONE LAKE
SNAKE RIVER
WYOMING

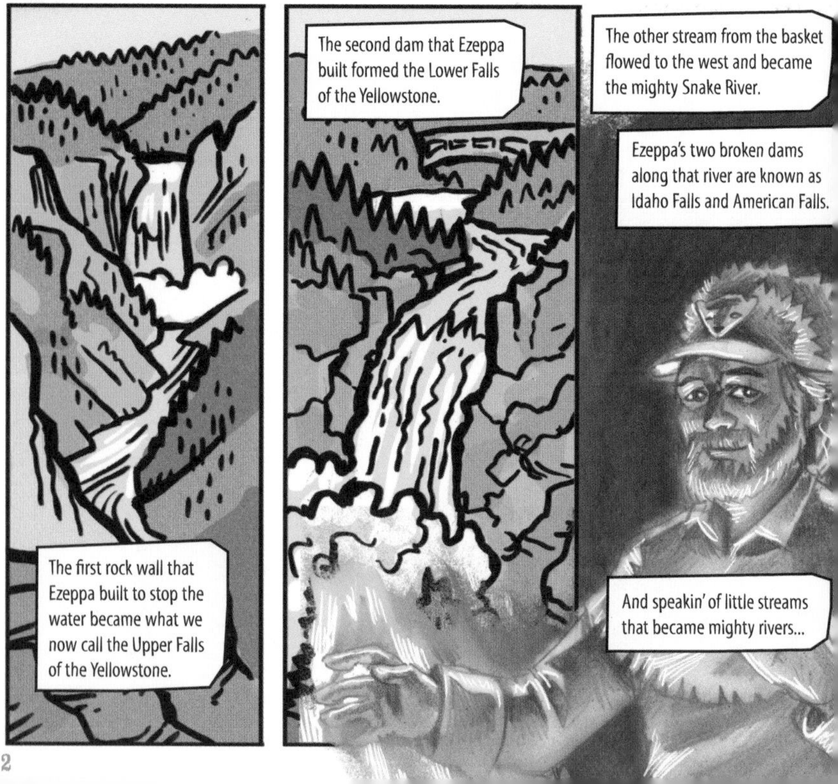
The first rock wall that Ezeppa built to stop the water became what we now call the Upper Falls of the Yellowstone.
The second dam that Ezeppa built formed the Lower Falls of the Yellowstone.
The other stream from the basket flowed to the west and became the mighty Snake River.
Ezeppa's two broken dams along that river are known as Idaho Falls and American Falls.
And speakin' of little streams that became mighty rivers...

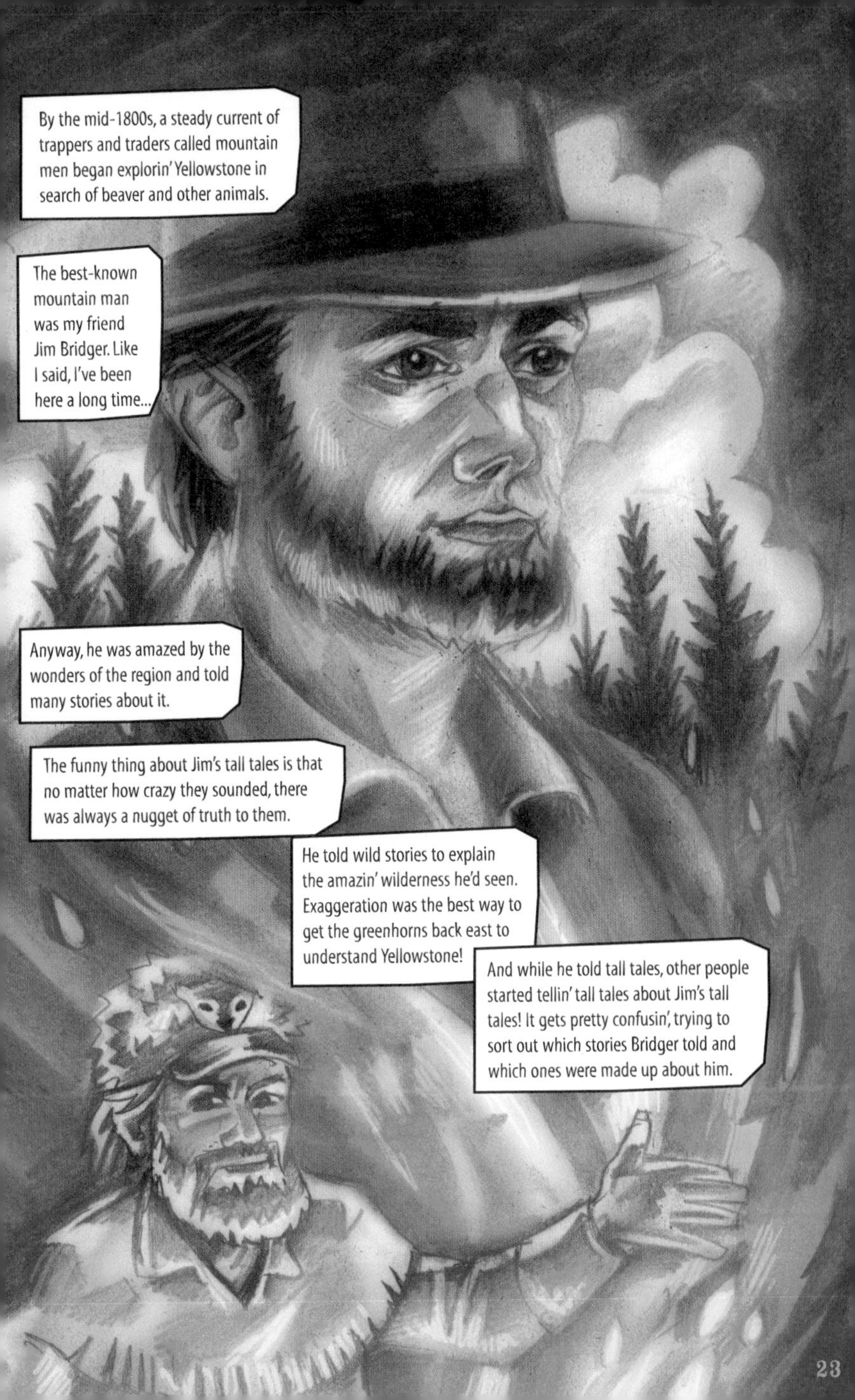

By the mid-1800s, a steady current of trappers and traders called mountain men began explorin' Yellowstone in search of beaver and other animals.
The best-known mountain man was my friend Jim Bridger. Like I said, I've been here a long time...
Anyway, he was amazed by the wonders of the region and told many stories about it.
The funny thing about Jim's tall tales is that no matter how crazy they sounded, there was always a nugget of truth to them.
He told wild stories to explain the amazin' wilderness he'd seen. Exaggeration was the best way to get the greenhorns back east to understand Yellowstone!
And while he told tall tales, other people started tellin' tall tales about Jim's tall tales! It gets pretty confusin', trying to sort out which stories Bridger told and which ones were made up about him.

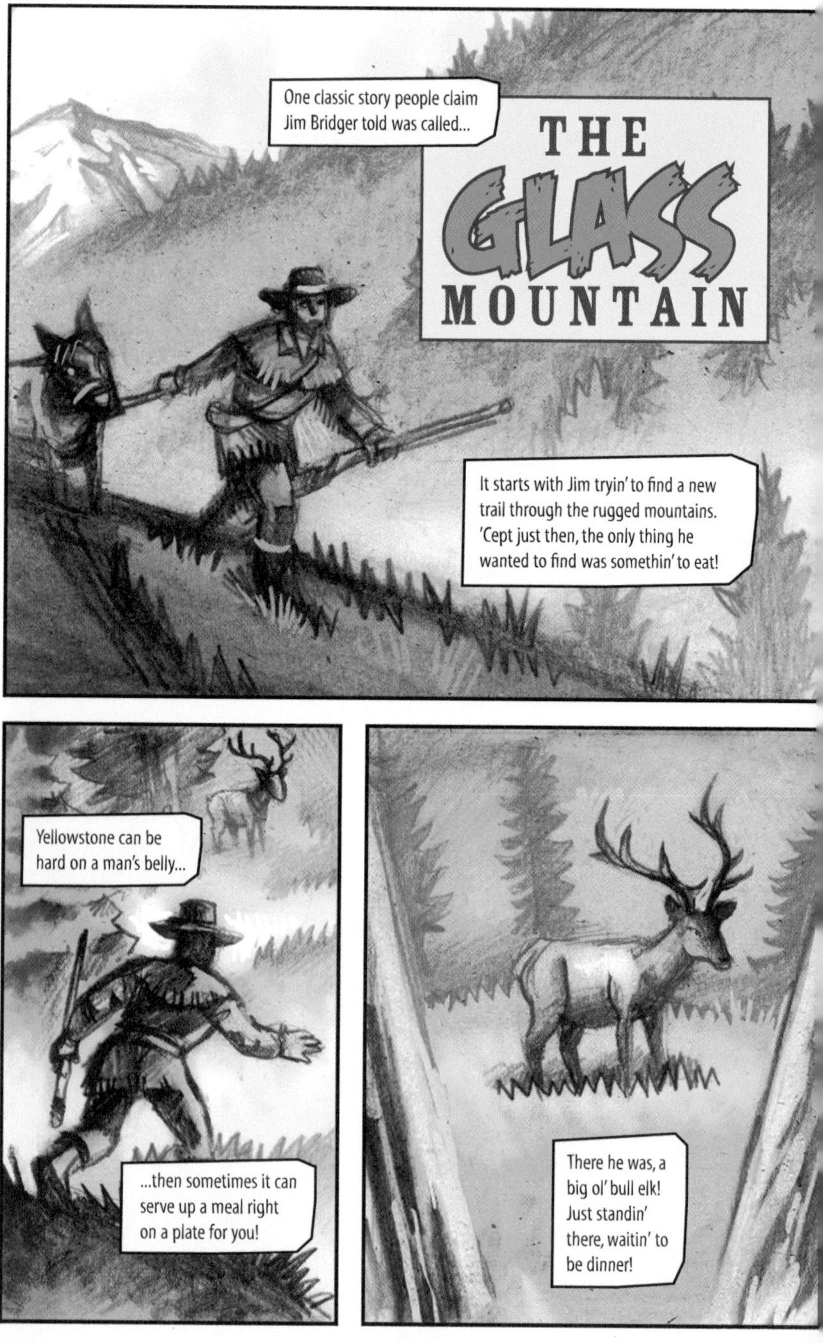

One classic story people claim
Jim Bridger told was called...
THE GLASS MOUNTAIN
It starts with Jim tryin' to find a new trail through the rugged mountains. 'Cept just then, the only thing he wanted to find was somethin' to eat!
Yellowstone can be hard on a man's belly...
...then sometimes it can serve up a meal right on a plate for you!
There he was, a big ol' bull elk! Just standin' there, waitin' to be dinner!

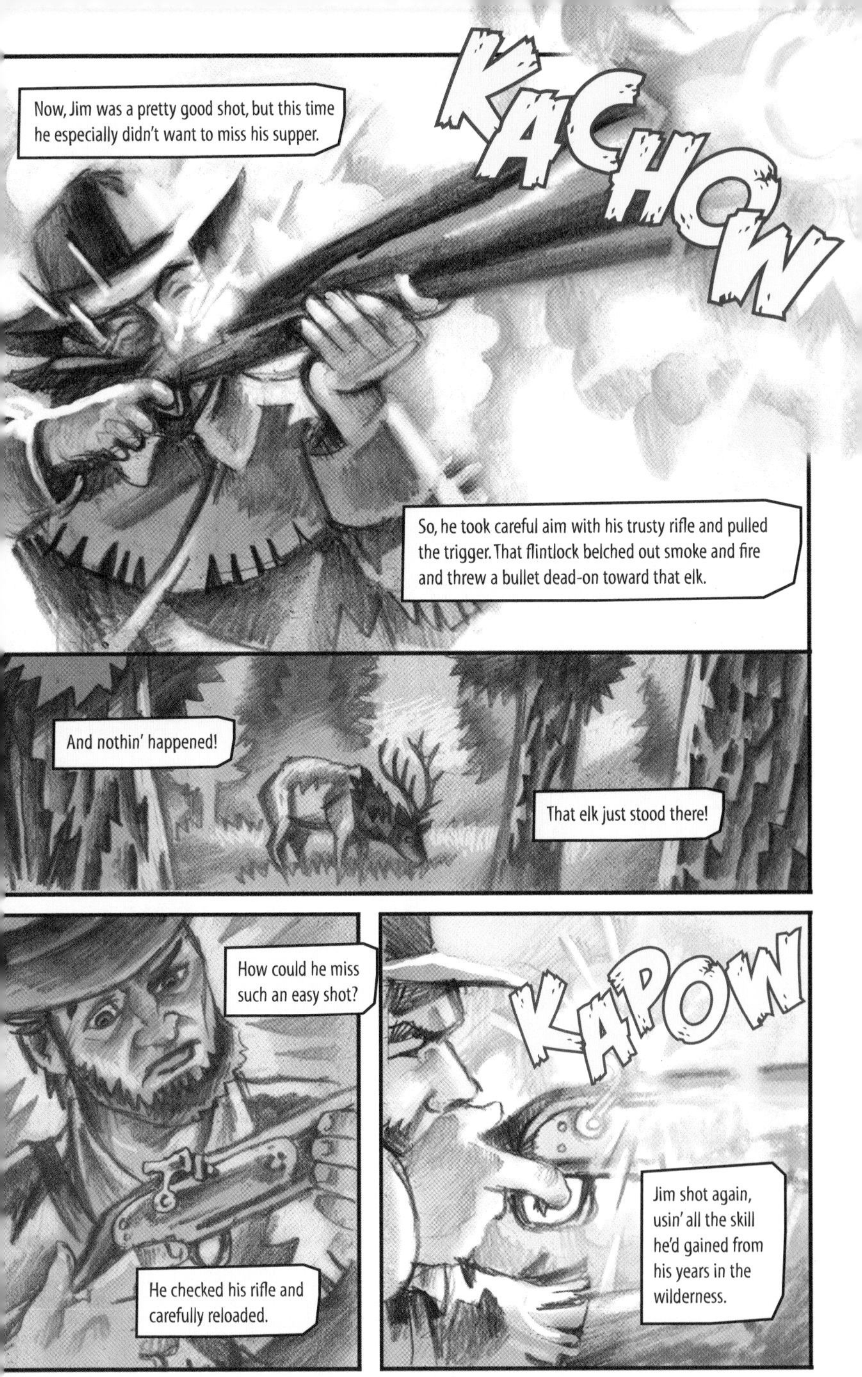
Now, Jim was a pretty good shot, but this time he especially didn't want to miss his supper.
KACHOW
So, he took careful aim with his trusty rifle and pulled the trigger. That flintlock belched out smoke and fire and threw a bullet dead-on toward that elk.
And nothin' happened!
That elk just stood there!
How could he miss such an easy shot?
He checked his rifle and carefully reloaded.
KAPOW
Jim shot again, usin' all the skill he'd gained from his years in the wilderness.

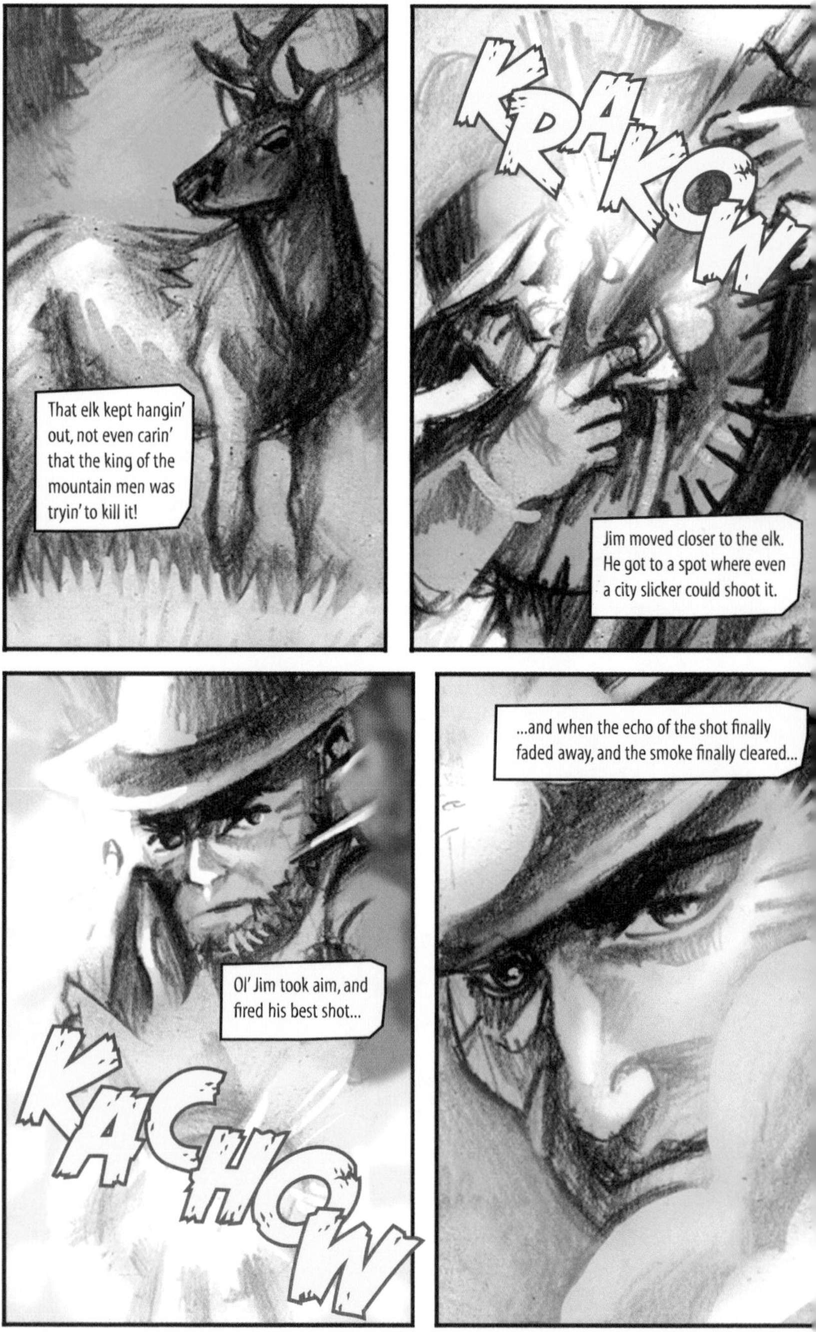
That elk kept hangin' out, not even carin' that the king of the mountain men was tryin' to kill it!
KRAKOW
Jim moved closer to the elk. He got to a spot where even a city slicker could shoot it.
Ol' Jim took aim, and fired his best shot...
KACHOW
...and when the echo of the shot finally faded away, and the smoke finally cleared...

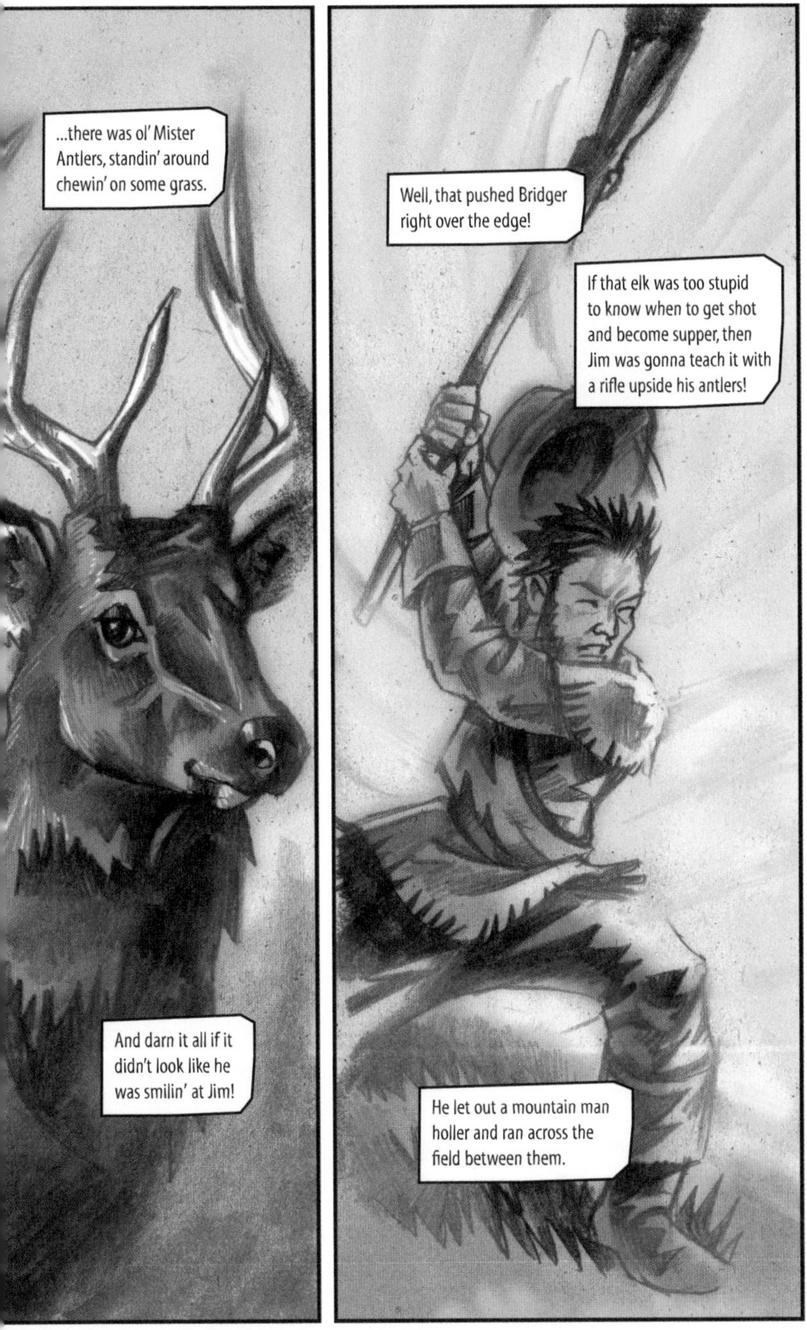
...there was ol' Mister Antlers, standin' around chewin' on some grass.
And darn it all if it didn't look like he was smilin' at Jim!
Well, that pushed Bridger right over the edge!
If that elk was too stupid to know when to get shot and become supper, then Jim was gonna teach it with a rifle upside his antlers!
He let out a mountain man holler and ran across the field between them.

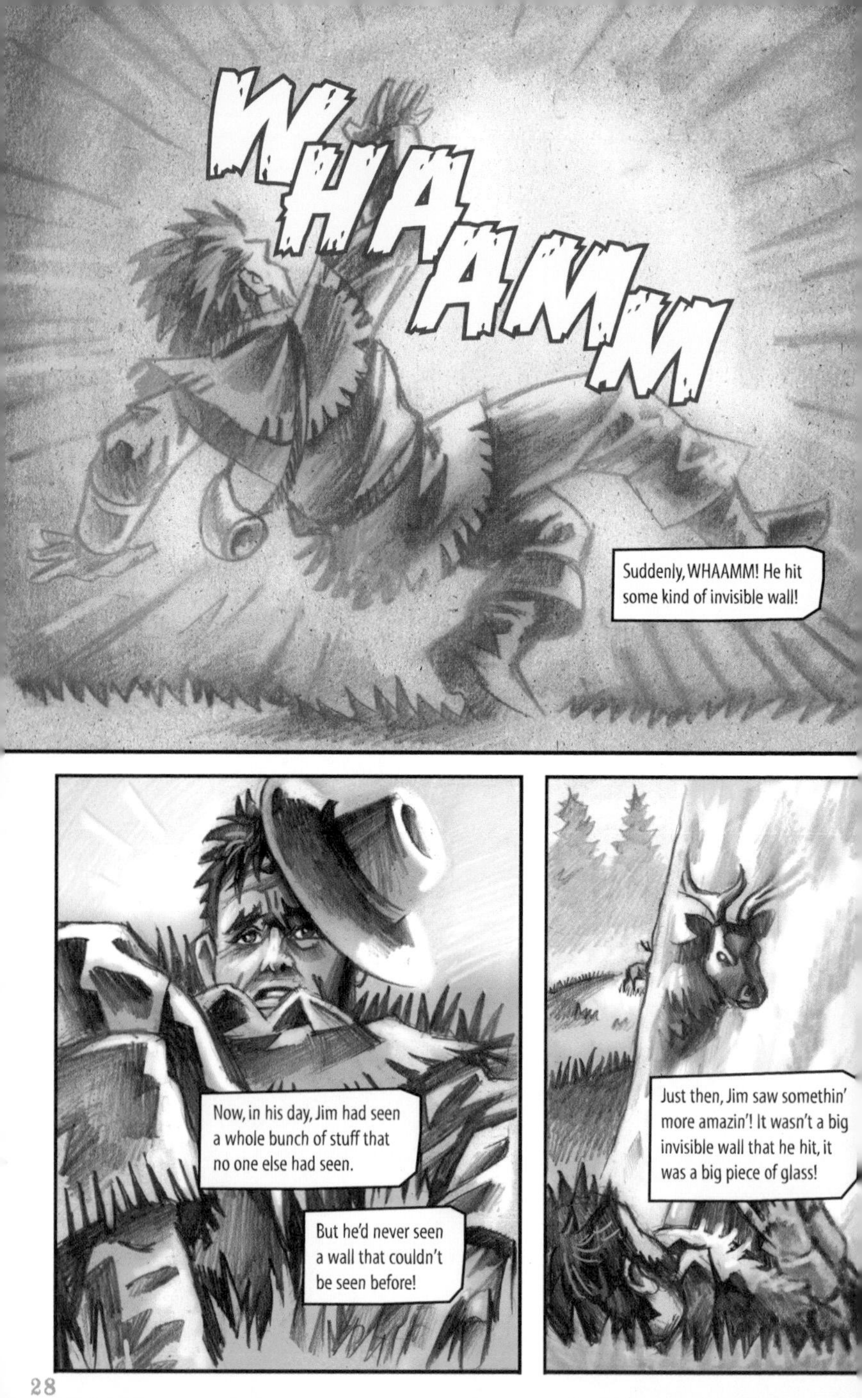
WHAAMM
Suddenly, WHAAMM! He hit some kind of invisible wall!
Now, in his day, Jim had seen a whole bunch of stuff that no one else had seen.
But he'd never seen a wall that couldn't be seen before!
Just then, Jim saw somethin' more amazin'! It wasn't a big invisible wall that he hit, it was a big piece of glass!

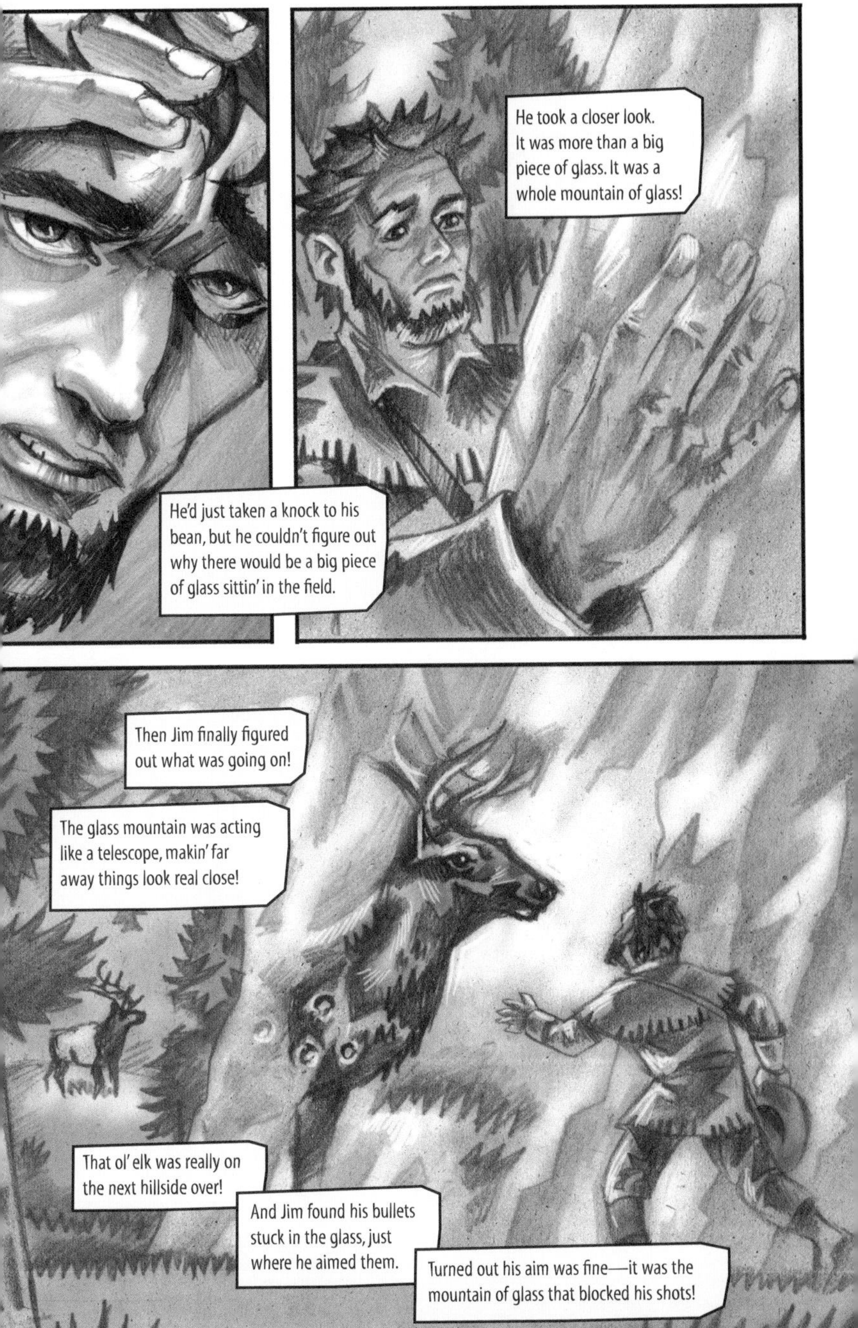
He'd just taken a knock to his bean, but he couldn't figure out why there would be a big piece of glass sittin' in the field.
He took a closer look. It was more than a big piece of glass. It was a whole mountain of glass!
Then Jim finally figured out what was going on!
The glass mountain was acting like a telescope, makin' far away things look real close!
That ol' elk was really on the next hillside over!
And Jim found his bullets stuck in the glass, just where he aimed them.
Turned out his aim was fine—it was the mountain of glass that blocked his shots!

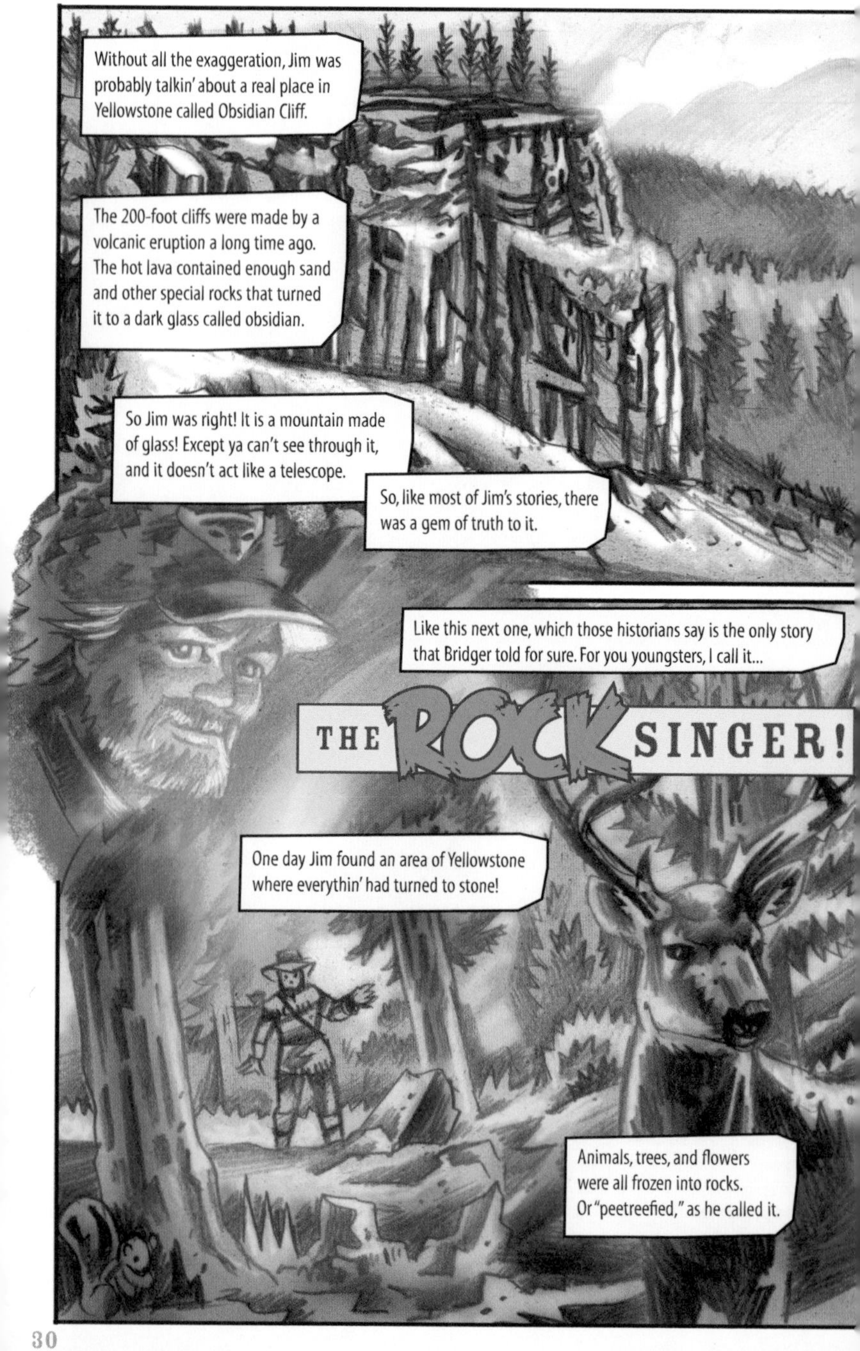
Without all the exaggeration, Jim was probably talkin' about a real place in Yellowstone called Obsidian Cliff.
The 200-foot cliffs were made by a volcanic eruption a long time ago. The hot lava contained enough sand and other special rocks that turned it to a dark glass called obsidian.
So Jim was right! It is a mountain made of glass! Except ya can't see through it, and it doesn't act like a telescope.
So, like most of Jim's stories, there was a gem of truth to it.
Like this next one, which those historians say is the only story that Bridger told for sure. For you youngsters, I call it...
THE ROCK SINGER!
One day Jim found an area of Yellowstone where everythin' had turned to stone!
Animals, trees, and flowers were all frozen into rocks. Or "peetreefied," as he called it.

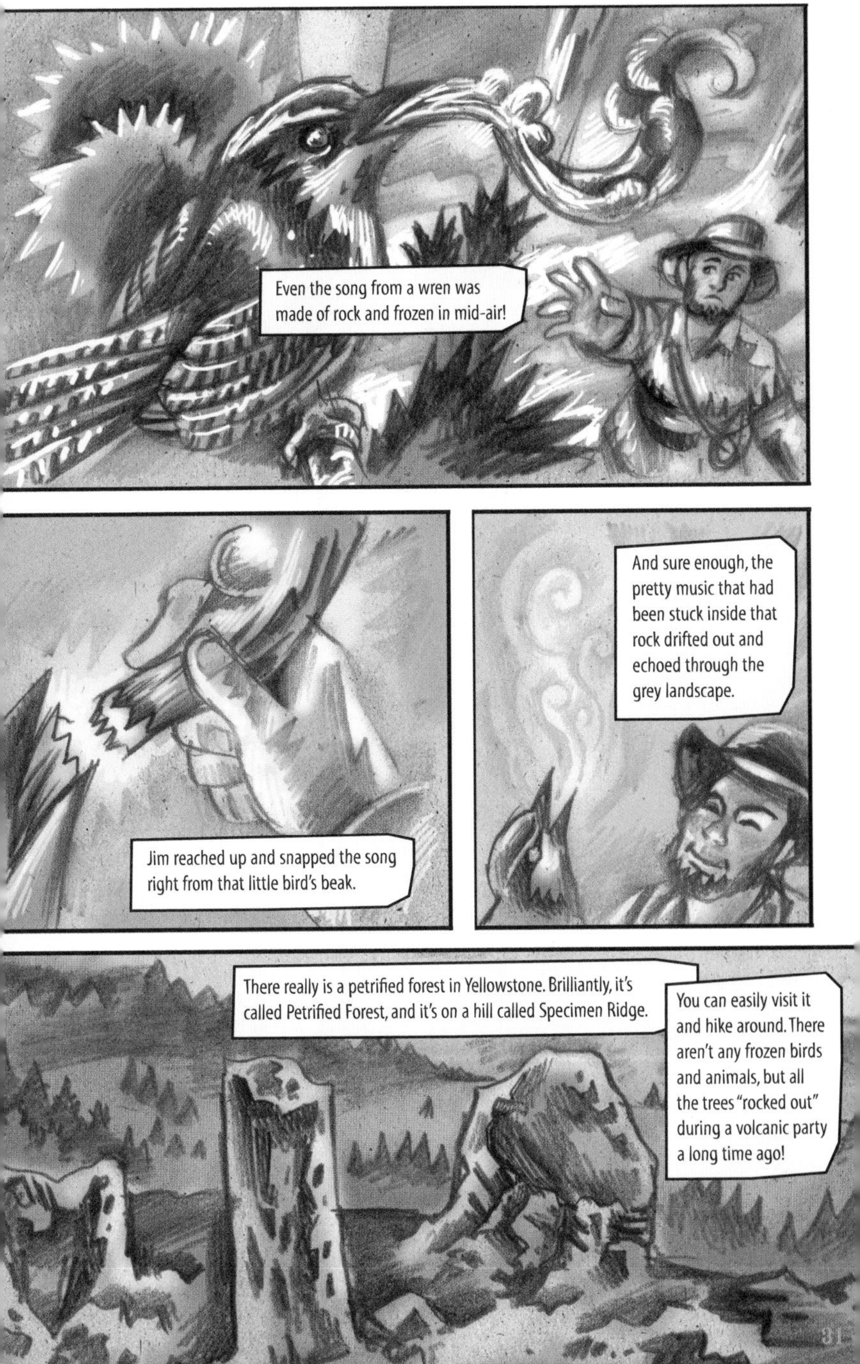
Even the song from a wren was made of rock and frozen in mid-air!
Jim reached up and snapped the song right from that little bird's beak.
And sure enough, the pretty music that had been stuck inside that rock drifted out and echoed through the grey landscape.
There really is a petrified forest in Yellowstone. Brilliantly, it's called Petrified Forest, and it's on a hill called Specimen Ridge.
You can easily visit it and hike around. There aren't any frozen birds and animals, but all the trees "rocked out" during a volcanic party a long time ago!

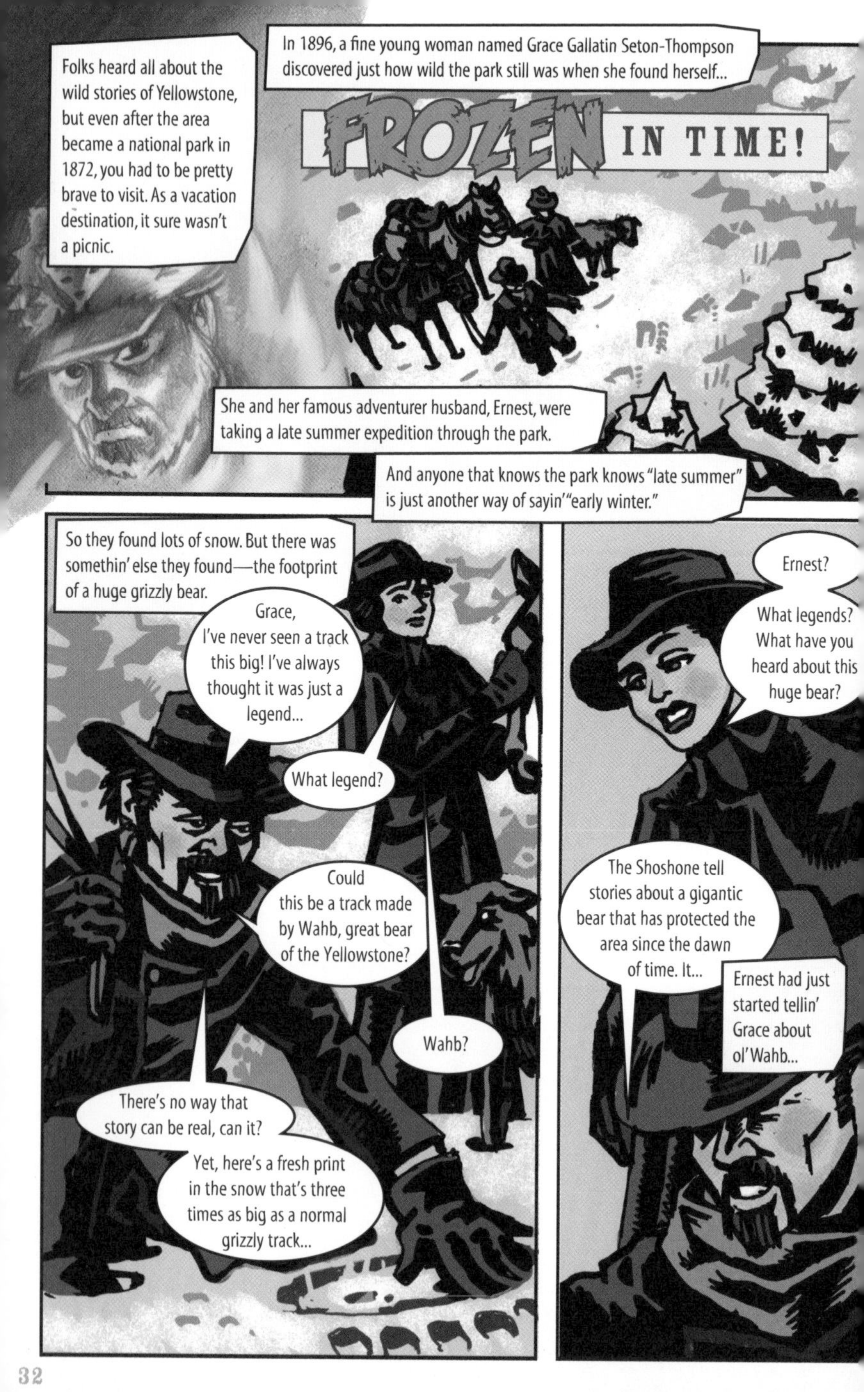
Folks heard all about the wild stories of Yellowstone, but even after the area became a national park in 1872, you had to be pretty brave to visit. As a vacation destination, it sure wasn't a picnic.
In 1896, a fine young woman named Grace Gallatin Seton-Thompson discovered just how wild the park still was when she found herself...
FROZEN IN TIME!
She and her famous adventurer husband, Ernest, were taking a late summer expedition through the park.
And anyone that knows the park knows "late summer" is just another way of sayin' "early winter."
So they found lots of snow. But there was somethin' else they found—the footprint of a huge grizzly bear.
Grace, I've never seen a track this big! I've always thought it was just a legend...
What legend?
Could this be a track made by Wahb, great bear of the Yellowstone?
Wahb?
There's no way that story can be real, can it?
Yet, here's a fresh print in the snow that's three times as big as a normal grizzly track...
Ernest?
What legends? What have you heard about this huge bear?
The Shoshone tell stories about a gigantic bear that has protected the area since the dawn of time. It...
Ernest had just started tellin' Grace about ol' Wahb...

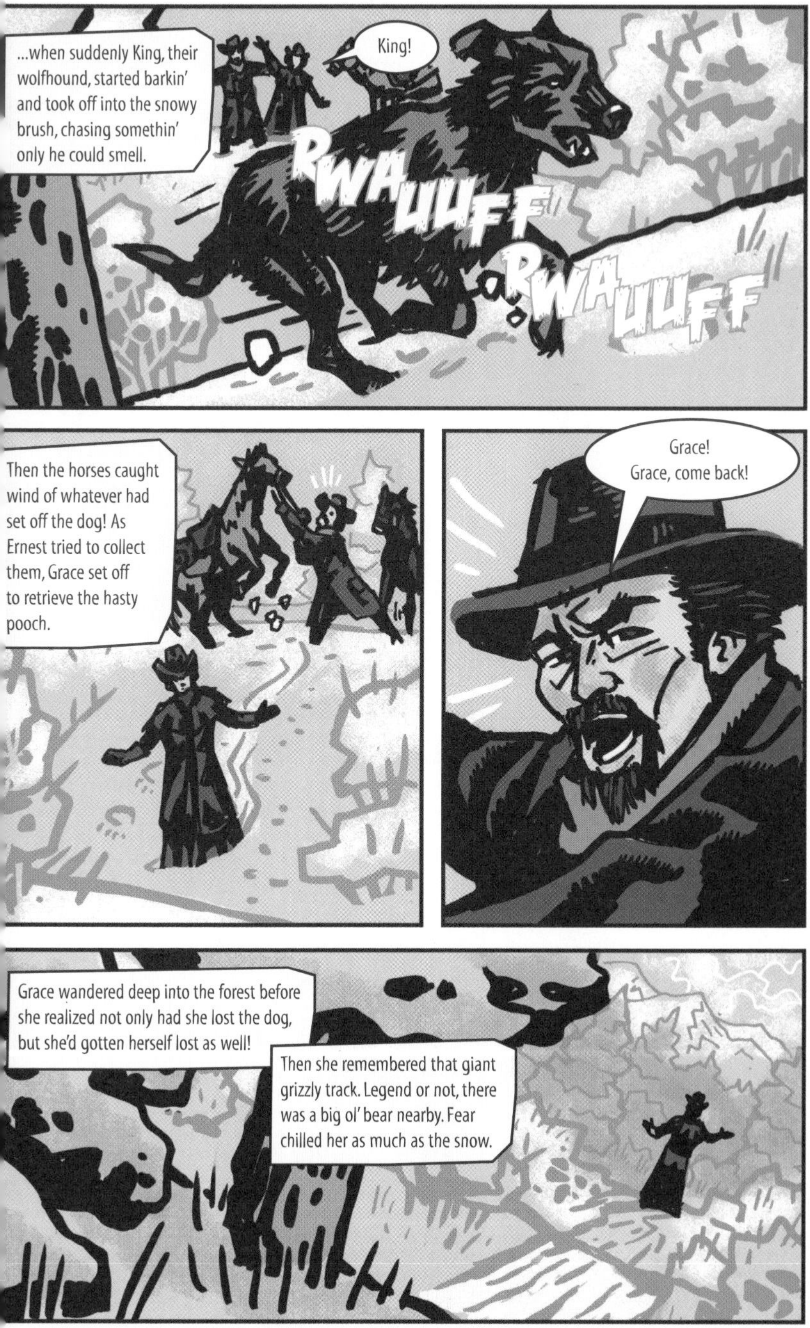
...when suddenly King, their wolfhound, started barkin' and took off into the snowy brush, chasing somethin' only he could smell.
King!
RWAUUFF
RWAUUFF
Then the horses caught wind of whatever had set off the dog! As Ernest tried to collect them, Grace set off to retrieve the hasty pooch.
Grace!
Grace, come back!
Grace wandered deep into the forest before she realized not only had she lost the dog, but she'd gotten herself lost as well!
Then she remembered that giant grizzly track. Legend or not, there was a big ol' bear nearby. Fear chilled her as much as the snow.

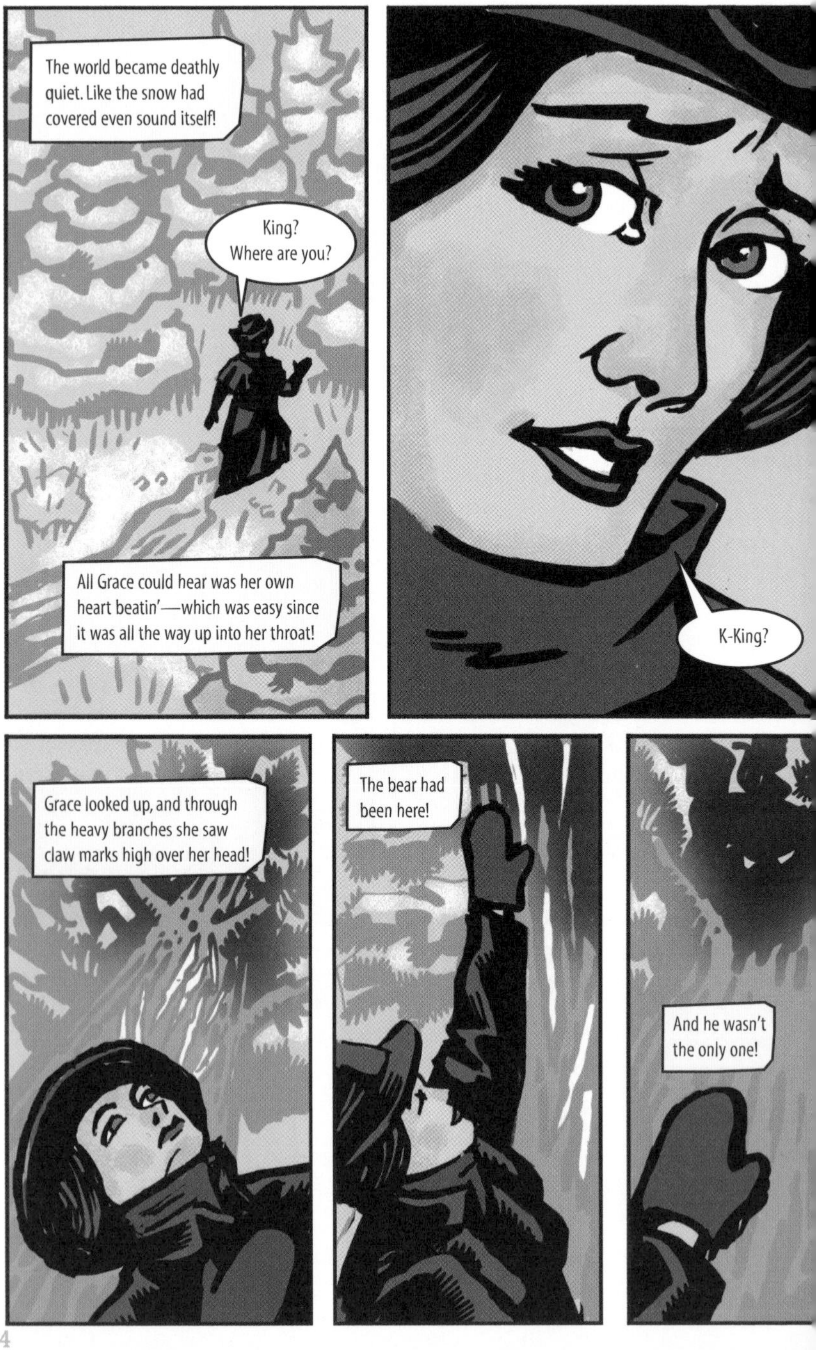
The world became deathly quiet. Like the snow had covered even sound itself!
King? Where are you?
All Grace could hear was her own heart beatin'—which was easy since it was all the way up into her throat!
K-King?
Grace looked up, and through the heavy branches she saw claw marks high over her head!
The bear had been here!
And he wasn't the only one!

RRNWRR

The quiet of the forest was shattered when she heard a terrible shriek from the tree above her!

There was a hungry bobcat, just waitin' to pounce!

Slowly, Grace backed up, tryin' to get away without causin' that kitty to strike!

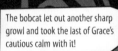

The bobcat let out another sharp growl and took the last of Grace's cautious calm with it!

RRNWRR

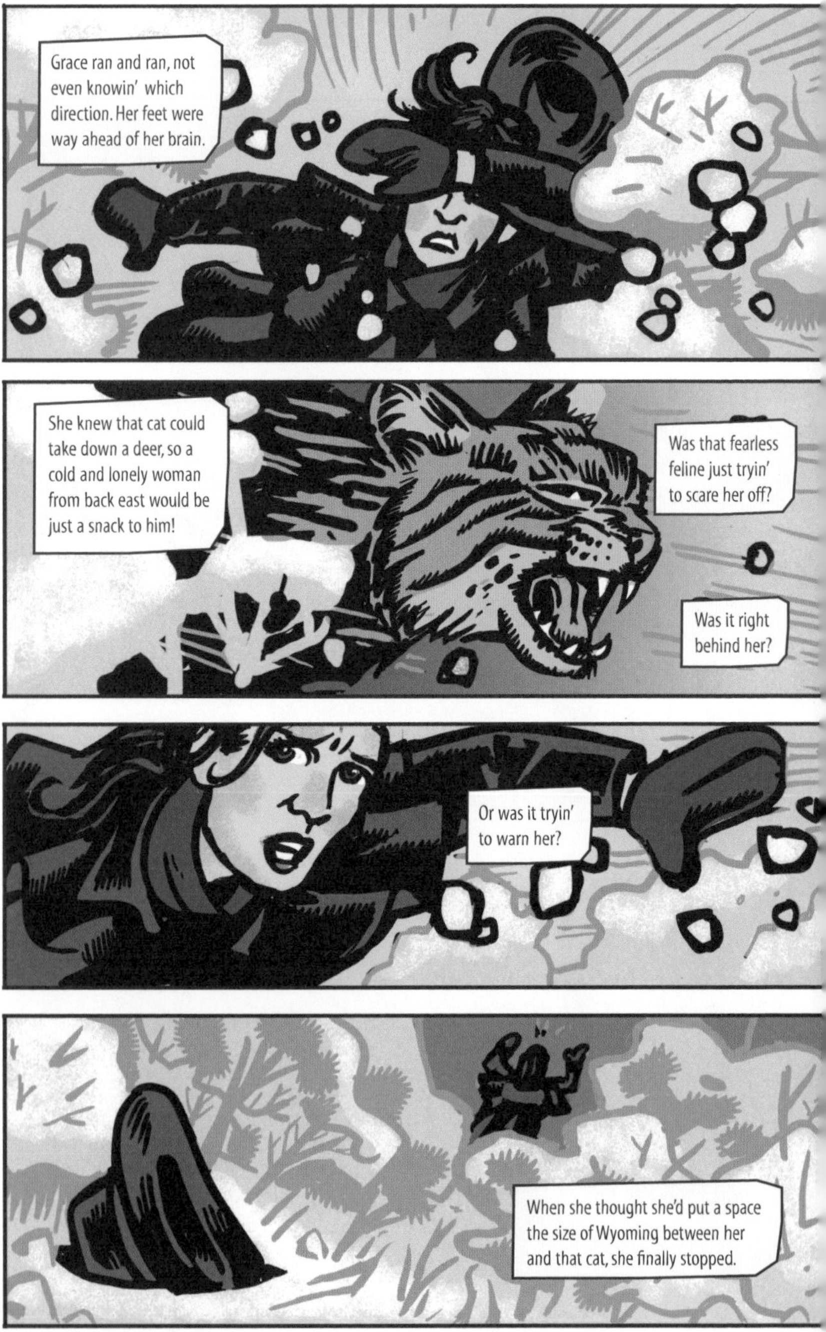
Grace ran and ran, not even knowin' which direction. Her feet were way ahead of her brain.
She knew that cat could take down a deer, so a cold and lonely woman from back east would be just a snack to him!
Was that fearless feline just tryin' to scare her off?
Was it right behind her?
Or was it tryin' to warn her?
When she thought she'd put a space the size of Wyoming between her and that cat, she finally stopped.

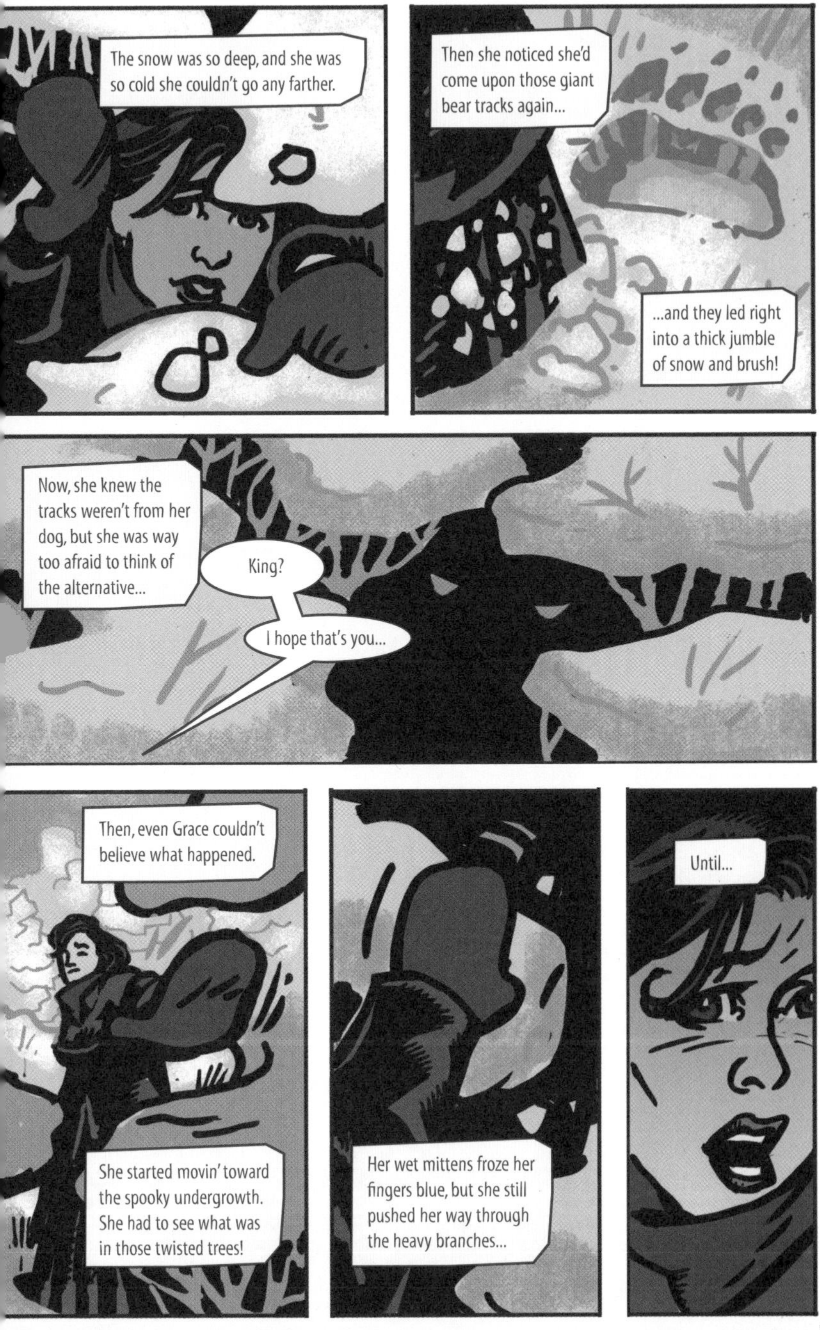
The snow was so deep, and she was so cold she couldn't go any farther.
Then she noticed she'd come upon those giant bear tracks again...
...and they led right into a thick jumble of snow and brush!
Now, she knew the tracks weren't from her dog, but she was way too afraid to think of the alternative...
King?
I hope that's you...
Then, even Grace couldn't believe what happened.
She started movin' toward the spooky undergrowth. She had to see what was in those twisted trees!
Her wet mittens froze her fingers blue, but she still pushed her way through the heavy branches...
Until...

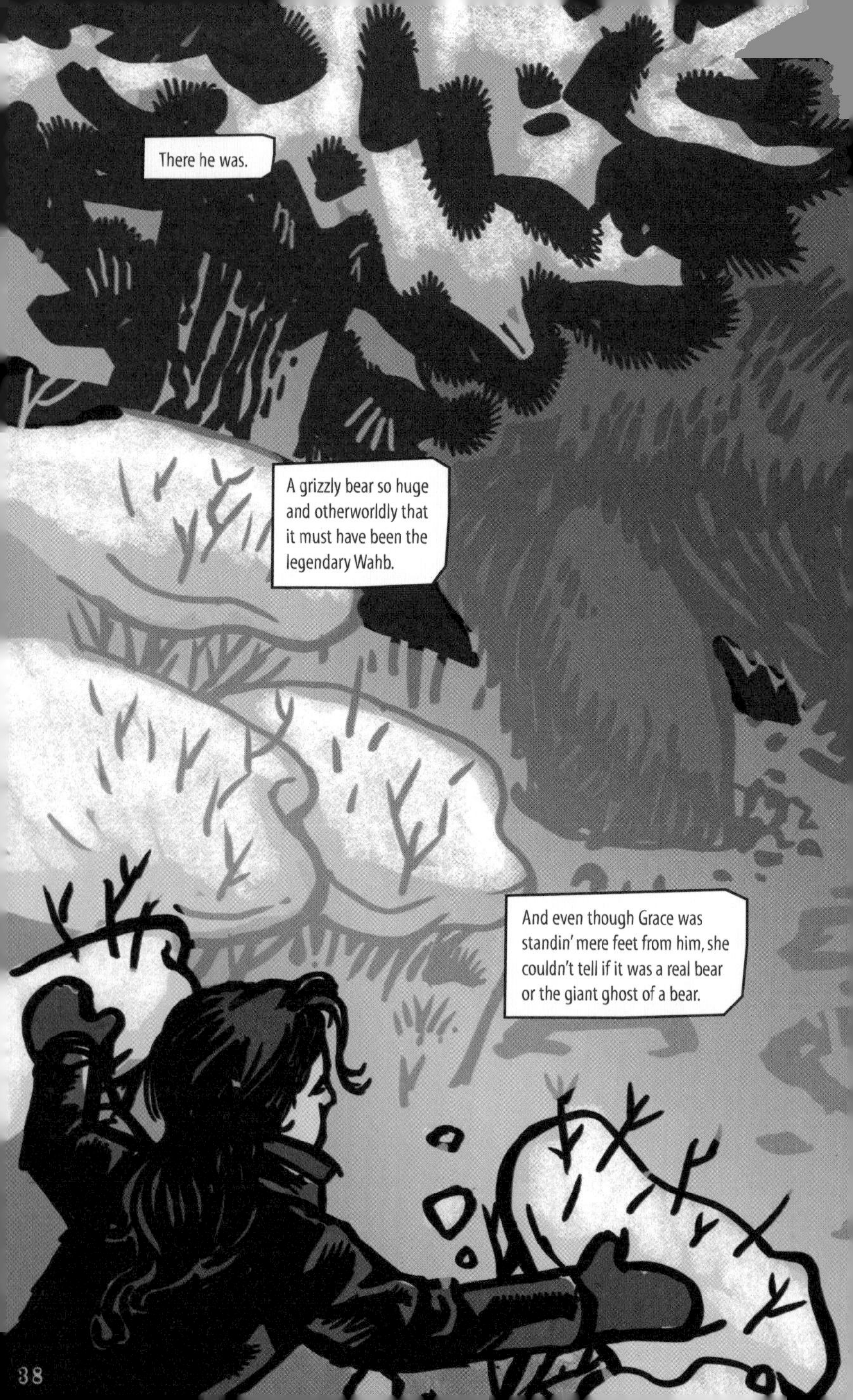
There he was.
A grizzly bear so huge and otherworldly that it must have been the legendary Wahb.
And even though Grace was standin' mere feet from him, she couldn't tell if it was a real bear or the giant ghost of a bear.

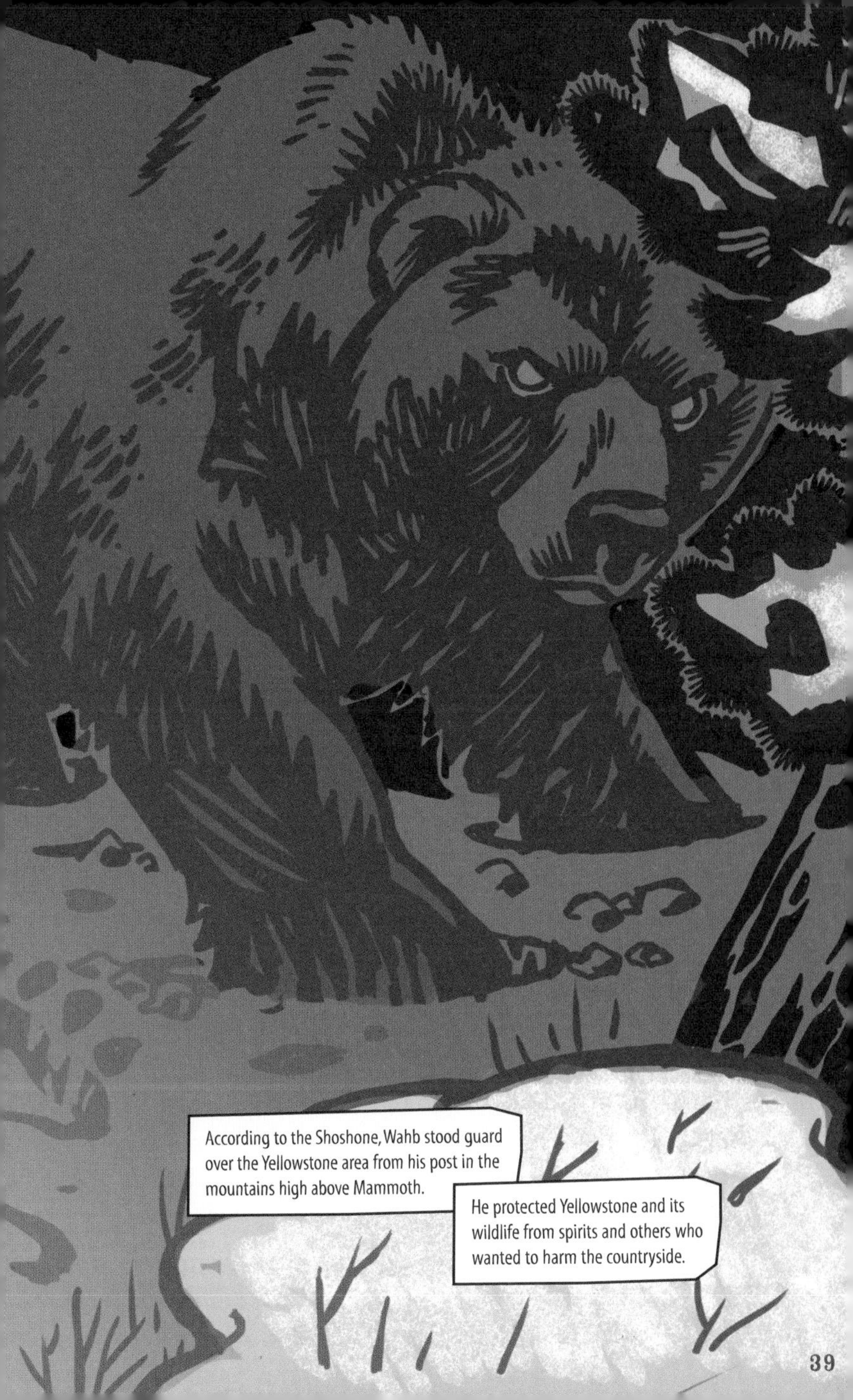
According to the Shoshone, Wahb stood guard over the Yellowstone area from his post in the mountains high above Mammoth.
He protected Yellowstone and its wildlife from spirits and others who wanted to harm the countryside.

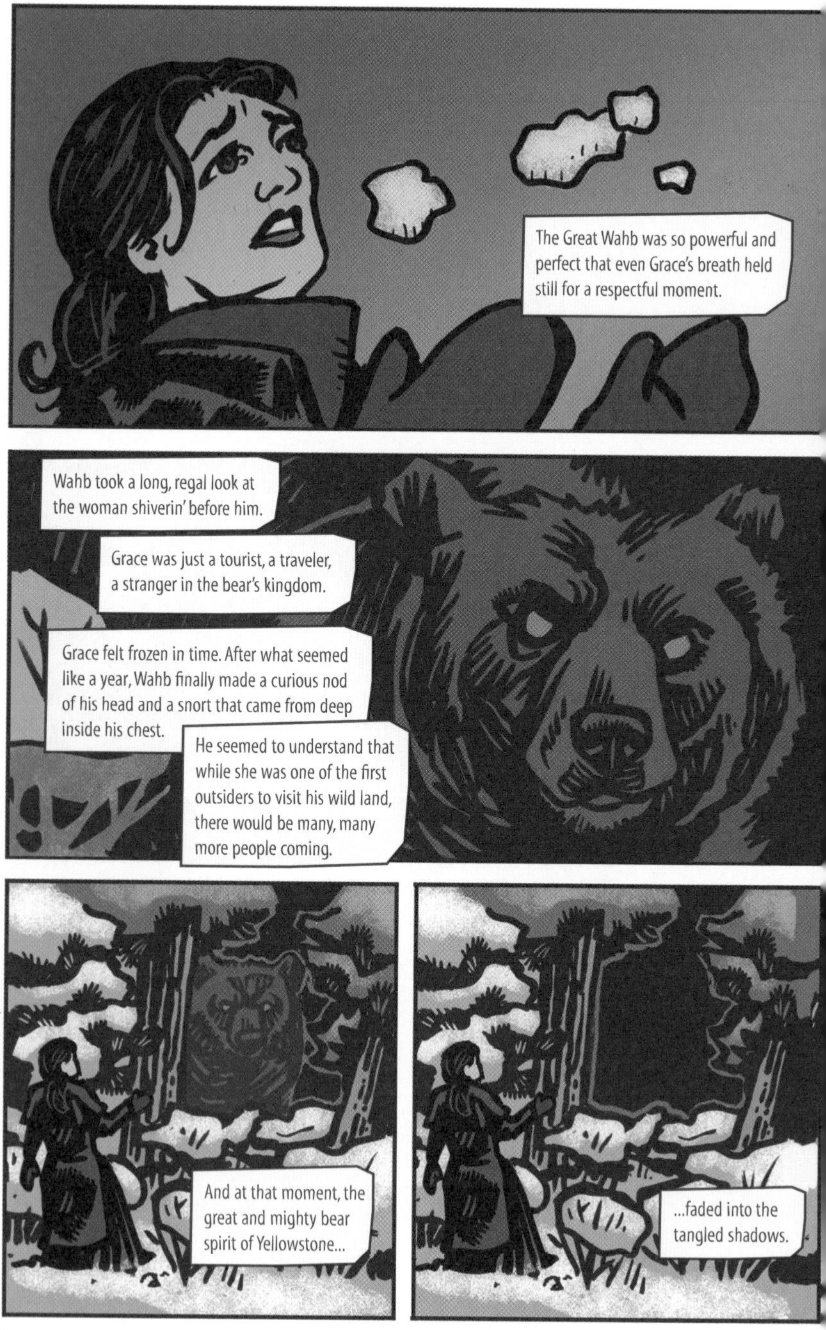
The Great Wahb was so powerful and perfect that even Grace's breath held still for a respectful moment.
Wahb took a long, regal look at the woman shiverin' before him.
Grace was just a tourist, a traveler, a stranger in the bear's kingdom.
Grace felt frozen in time. After what seemed like a year, Wahb finally made a curious nod of his head and a snort that came from deep inside his chest.
He seemed to understand that while she was one of the first outsiders to visit his wild land, there would be many, many more people coming.
And at that moment, the great and mighty bear spirit of Yellowstone...
...faded into the tangled shadows.

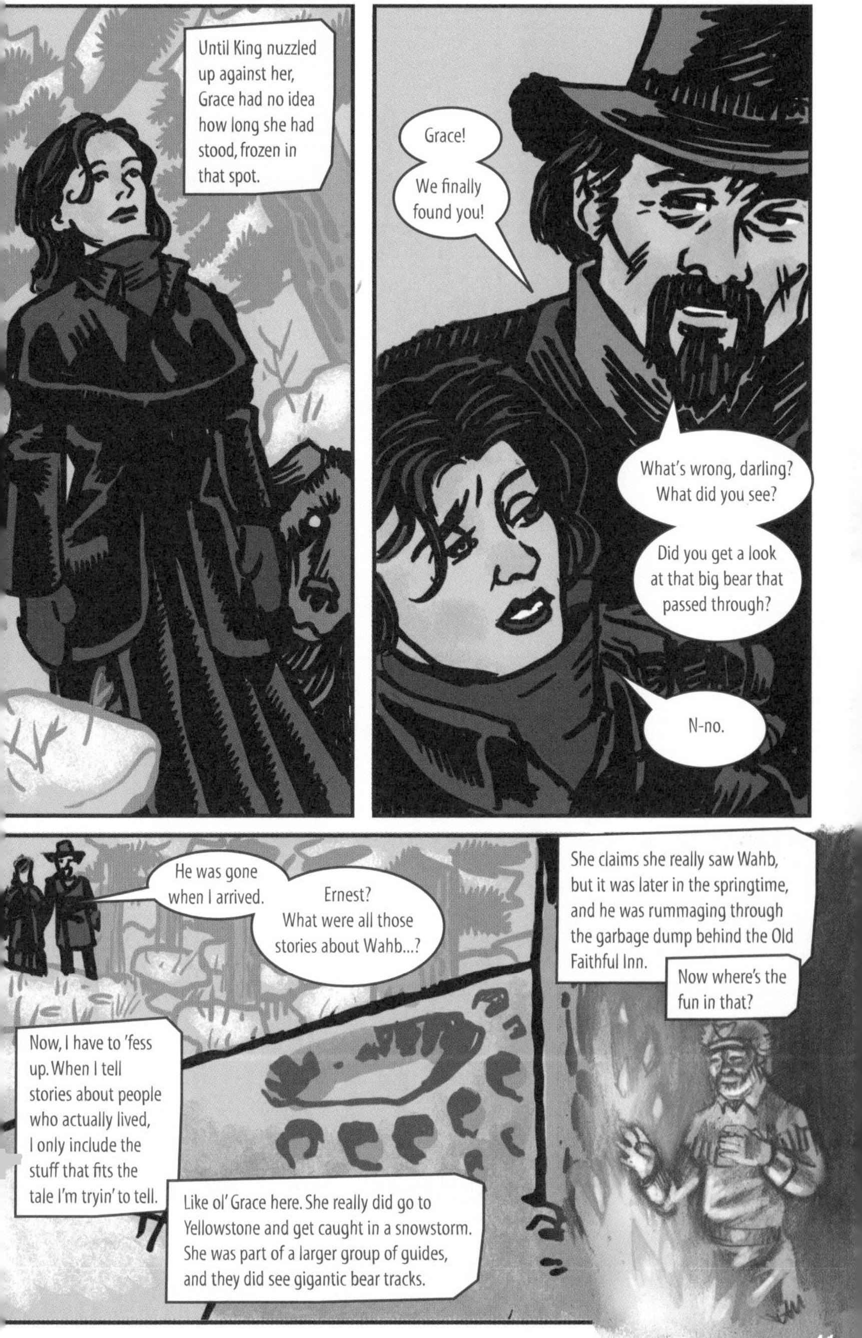
Until King nuzzled up against her, Grace had no idea how long she had stood, frozen in that spot.
Grace!
We finally found you!
What's wrong, darling? What did you see?
Did you get a look at that big bear that passed through?
N-no.
He was gone when I arrived.
Ernest? What were all those stories about Wahb...?
Now, I have to 'fess up. When I tell stories about people who actually lived, I only include the stuff that fits the tale I'm tryin' to tell.
Like ol' Grace here. She really did go to Yellowstone and get caught in a snowstorm. She was part of a larger group of guides, and they did see gigantic bear tracks.
She claims she really saw Wahb, but it was later in the springtime, and he was rummaging through the garbage dump behind the Old Faithful Inn.
Now where's the fun in that?

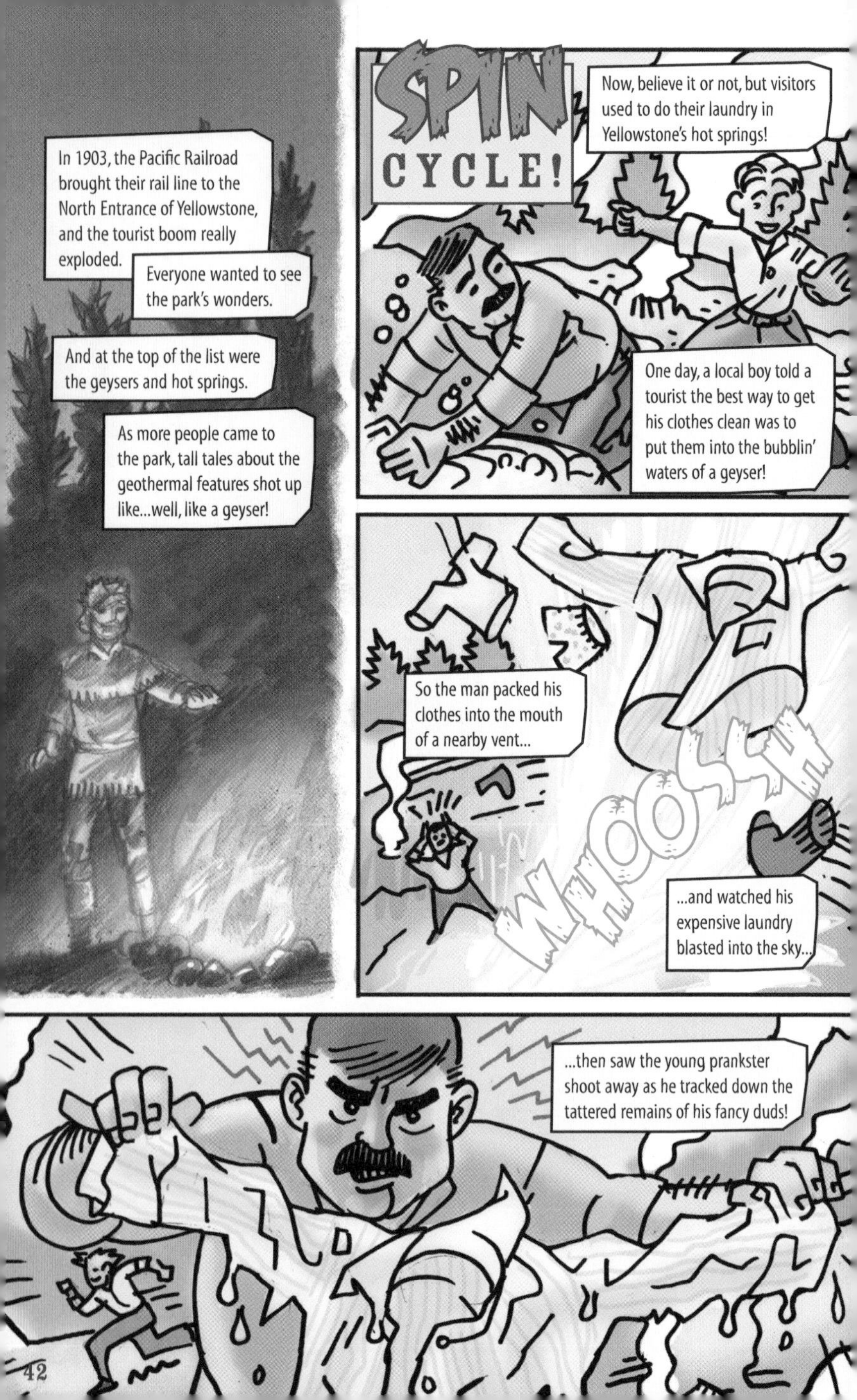
In 1903, the Pacific Railroad brought their rail line to the North Entrance of Yellowstone, and the tourist boom really exploded.
Everyone wanted to see the park's wonders.
And at the top of the list were the geysers and hot springs.
As more people came to the park, tall tales about the geothermal features shot up like...well, like a geyser!
SPIN CYCLE!
Now, believe it or not, but visitors used to do their laundry in Yellowstone's hot springs!
One day, a local boy told a tourist the best way to get his clothes clean was to put them into the bubblin' waters of a geyser!
So the man packed his clothes into the mouth of a nearby vent...
WHOOSH
...and watched his expensive laundry blasted into the sky...
...then saw the young prankster shoot away as he tracked down the tattered remains of his fancy duds!

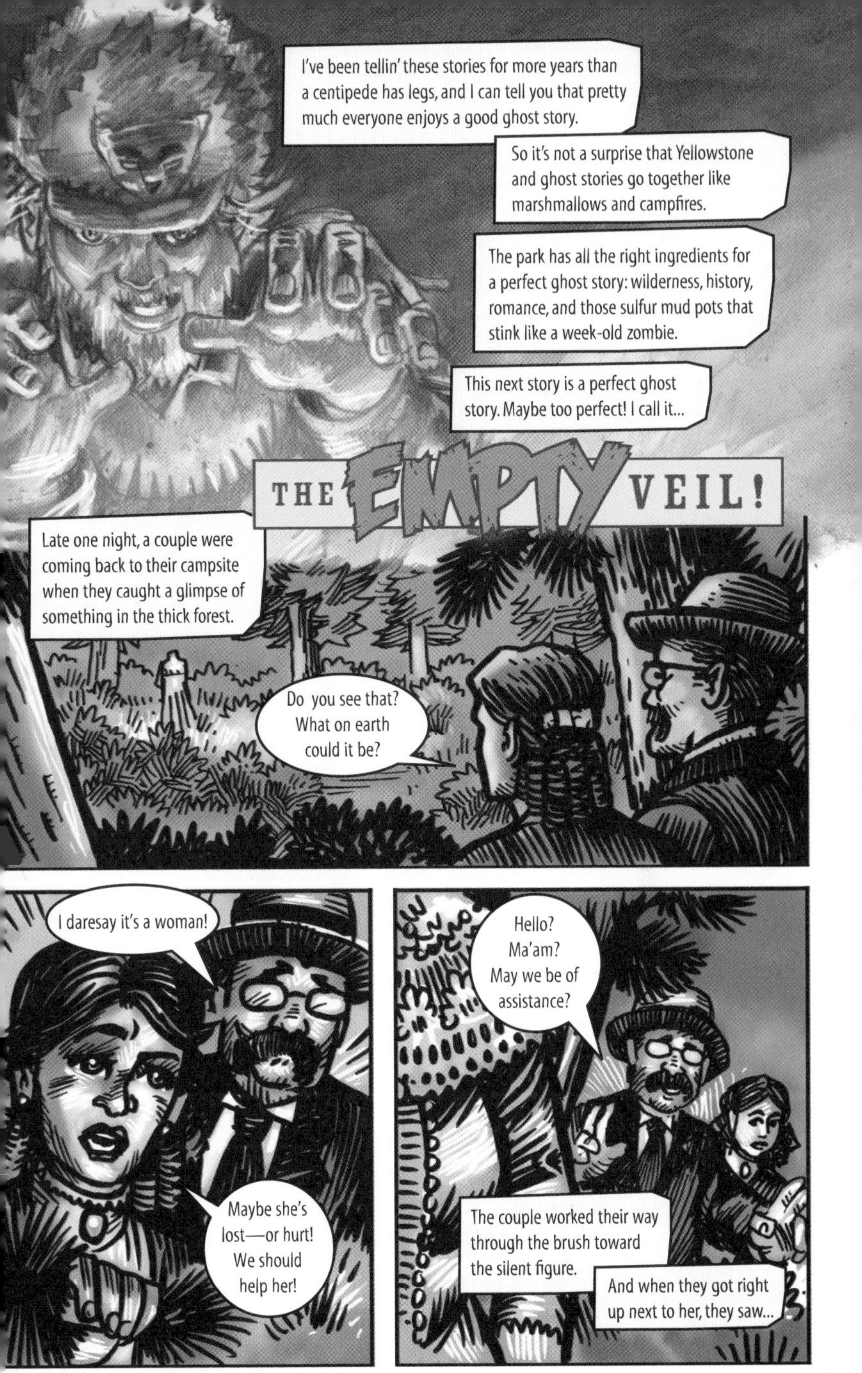
I've been tellin' these stories for more years than a centipede has legs, and I can tell you that pretty much everyone enjoys a good ghost story.
So it's not a surprise that Yellowstone and ghost stories go together like marshmallows and campfires.
The park has all the right ingredients for a perfect ghost story: wilderness, history, romance, and those sulfur mud pots that stink like a week-old zombie.
This next story is a perfect ghost story. Maybe too perfect! I call it...
THE EMPTY VEIL!
Late one night, a couple were coming back to their campsite when they caught a glimpse of something in the thick forest.
Do you see that? What on earth could it be?
I daresay it's a woman!
Maybe she's lost—or hurt! We should help her!
Hello? Ma'am? May we be of assistance?
The couple worked their way through the brush toward the silent figure.
And when they got right up next to her, they saw...

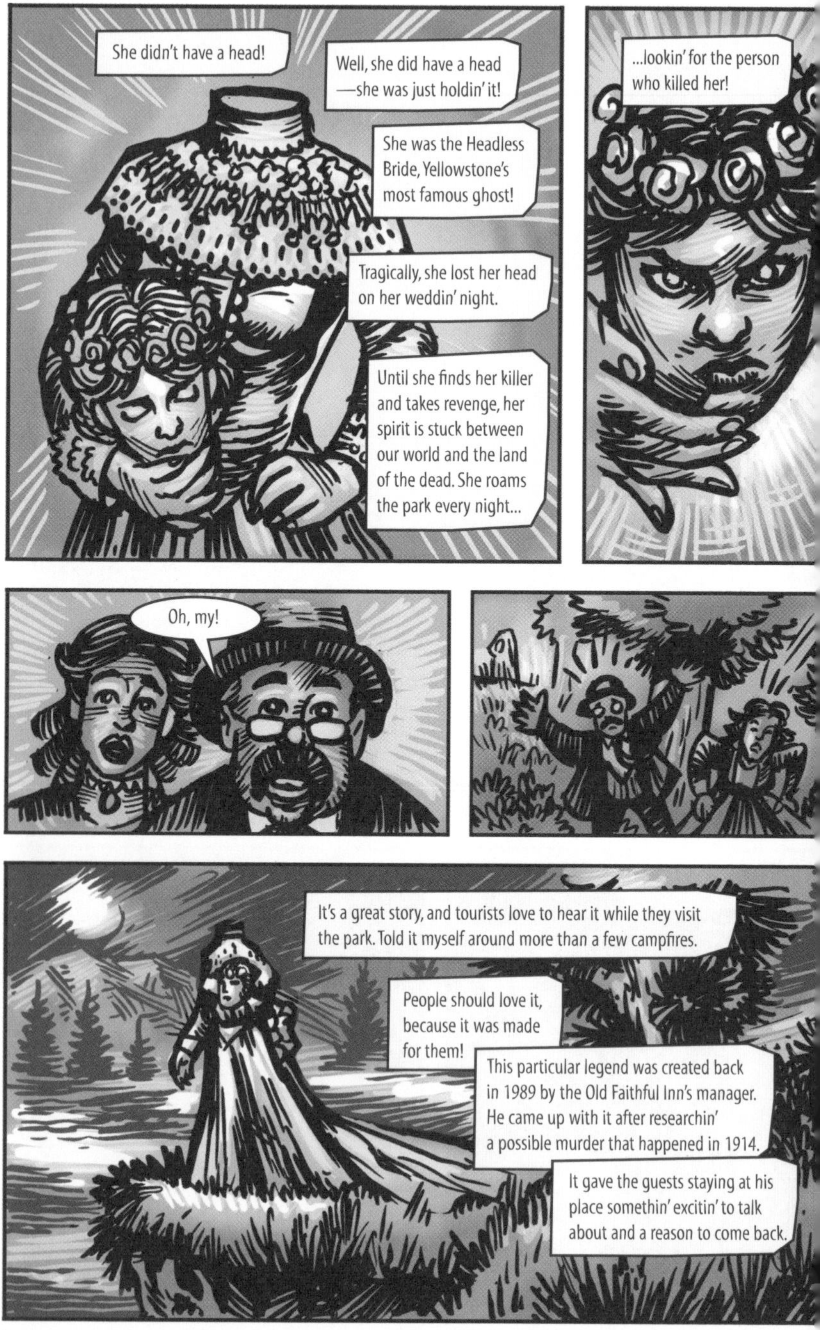
She didn't have a head!
Well, she did have a head —she was just holdin' it!
She was the Headless Bride, Yellowstone's most famous ghost!
Tragically, she lost her head on her weddin' night.
Until she finds her killer and takes revenge, her spirit is stuck between our world and the land of the dead. She roams the park every night...
...lookin' for the person who killed her!
Oh, my!
It's a great story, and tourists love to hear it while they visit the park. Told it myself around more than a few campfires.
People should love it, because it was made for them!
This particular legend was created back in 1989 by the Old Faithful Inn's manager. He came up with it after researchin' a possible murder that happened in 1914.
It gave the guests staying at his place somethin' excitin' to talk about and a reason to come back.

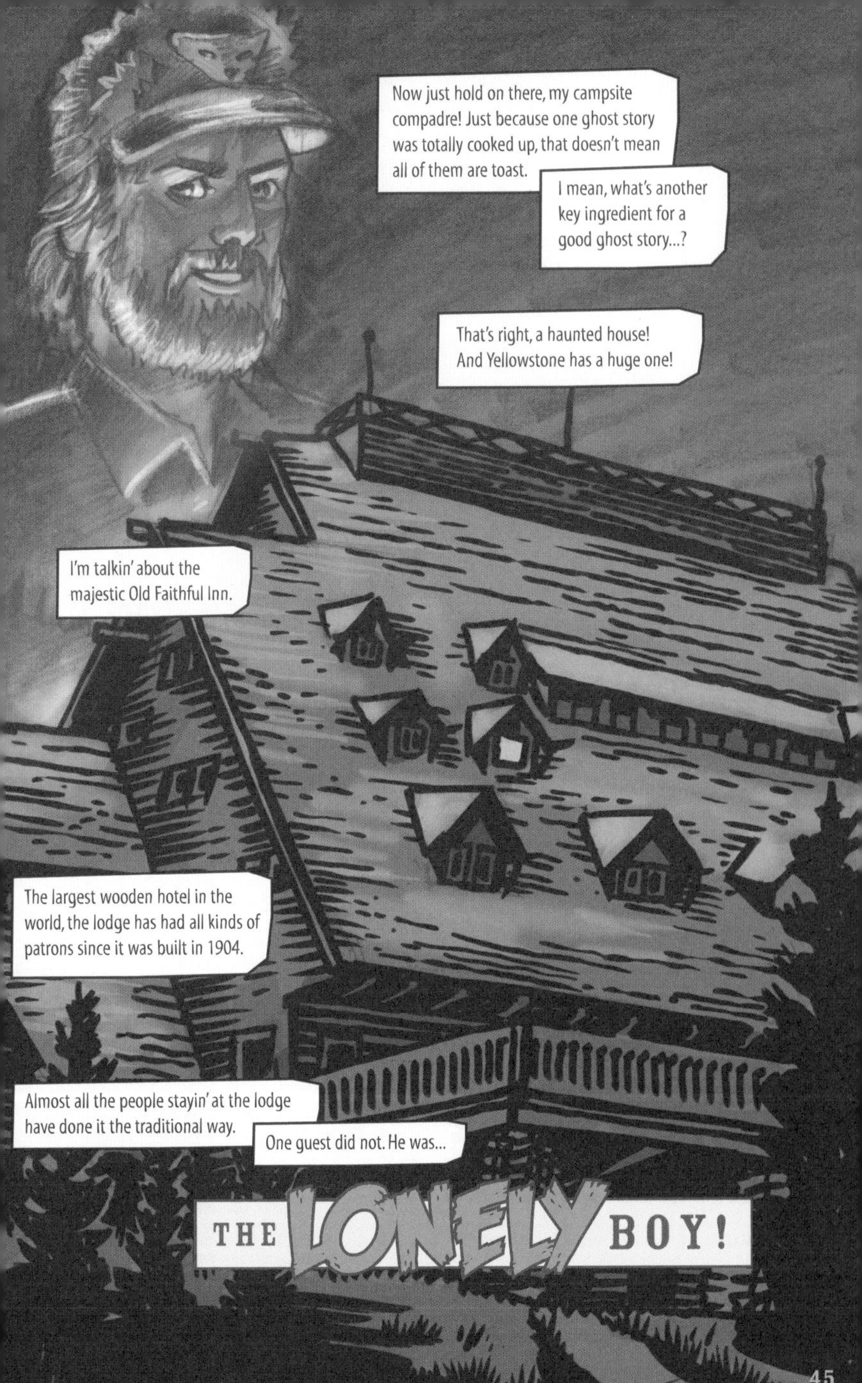
Now just hold on there, my campsite compadre! Just because one ghost story was totally cooked up, that doesn't mean all of them are toast.
I mean, what's another key ingredient for a good ghost story...?
That's right, a haunted house! And Yellowstone has a huge one!
I'm talkin' about the majestic Old Faithful Inn.
The largest wooden hotel in the world, the lodge has had all kinds of patrons since it was built in 1904.
Almost all the people stayin' at the lodge have done it the traditional way.
One guest did not. He was...
THE LONELY BOY!

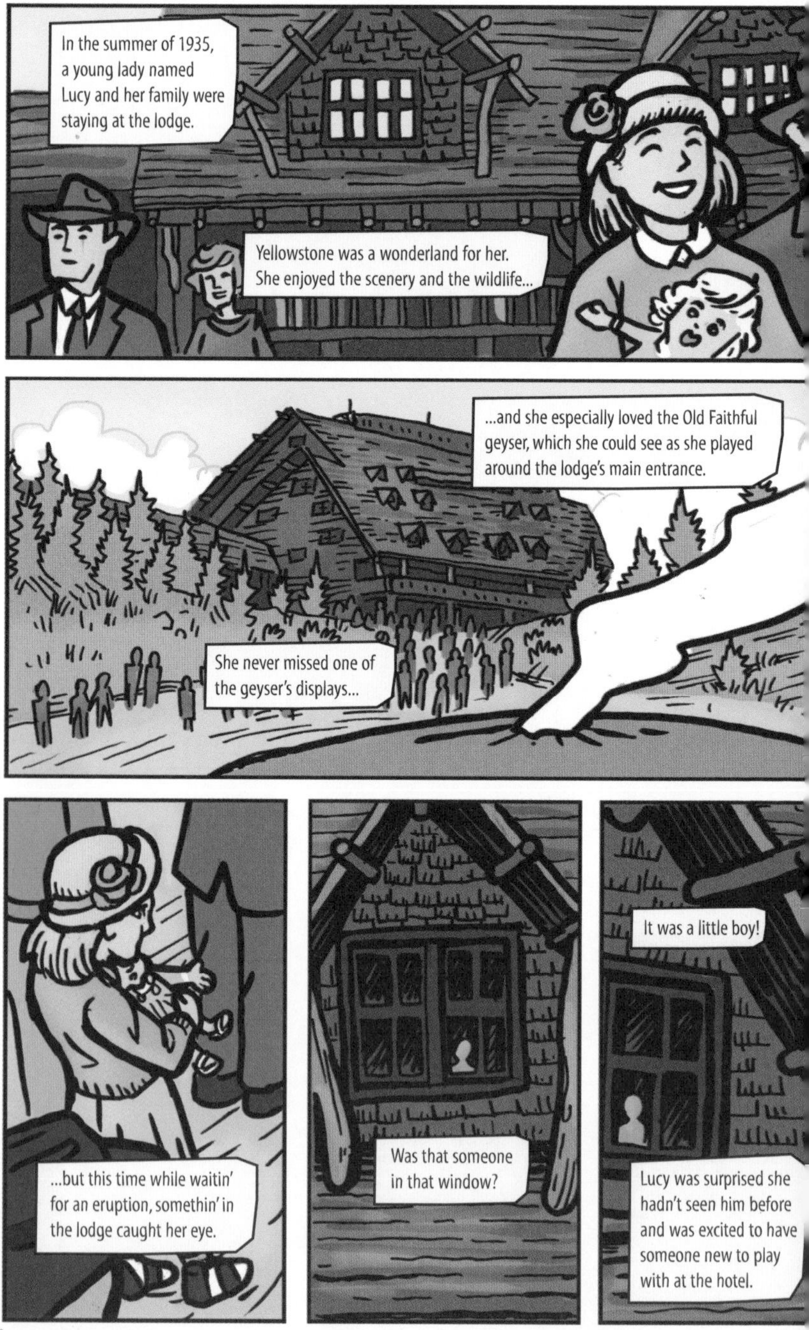
In the summer of 1935, a young lady named Lucy and her family were staying at the lodge.
Yellowstone was a wonderland for her. She enjoyed the scenery and the wildlife...
...and she especially loved the Old Faithful geyser, which she could see as she played around the lodge's main entrance.
She never missed one of the geyser's displays...
...but this time while waitin' for an eruption, somethin' in the lodge caught her eye.
Was that someone in that window?
It was a little boy!
Lucy was surprised she hadn't seen him before and was excited to have someone new to play with at the hotel.

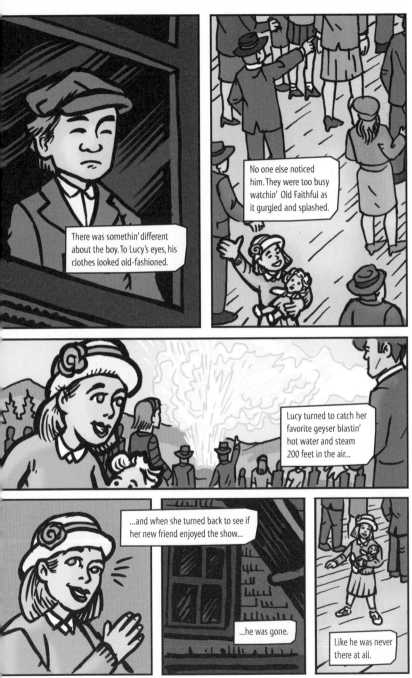

There was somethin' different about the boy. To Lucy's eyes, his clothes looked old-fashioned.

No one else noticed him. They were too busy watchin' Old Faithful as it gurgled and splashed.

Lucy turned to catch her favorite geyser blastin' hot water and steam 200 feet in the air...

...and when she turned back to see if her new friend enjoyed the show...

...he was gone.

Like he was never there at all.

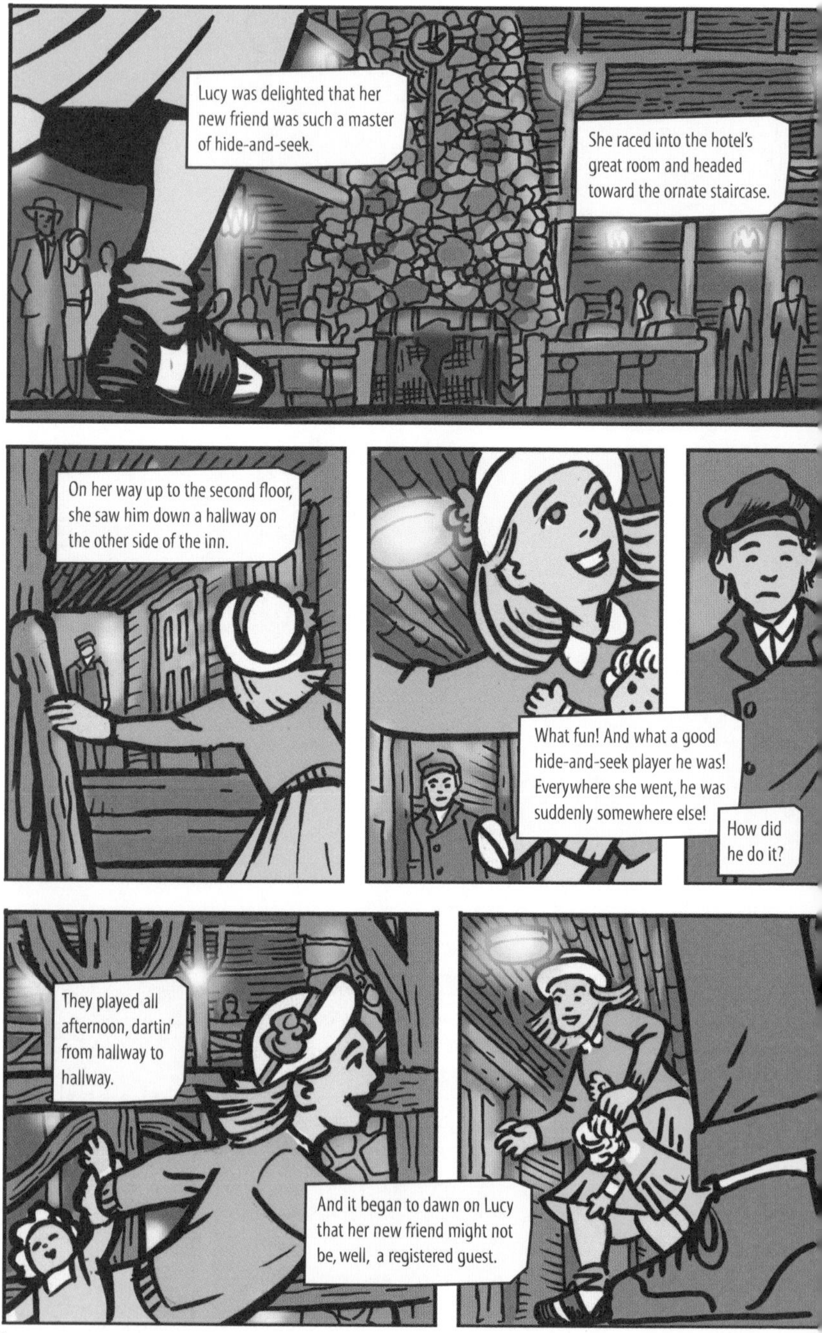
Lucy was delighted that her new friend was such a master of hide-and-seek.
She raced into the hotel's great room and headed toward the ornate staircase.
On her way up to the second floor, she saw him down a hallway on the other side of the inn.
What fun! And what a good hide-and-seek player he was! Everywhere she went, he was suddenly somewhere else!
How did he do it?
They played all afternoon, dartin' from hallway to hallway.
And it began to dawn on Lucy that her new friend might not be, well, a registered guest.

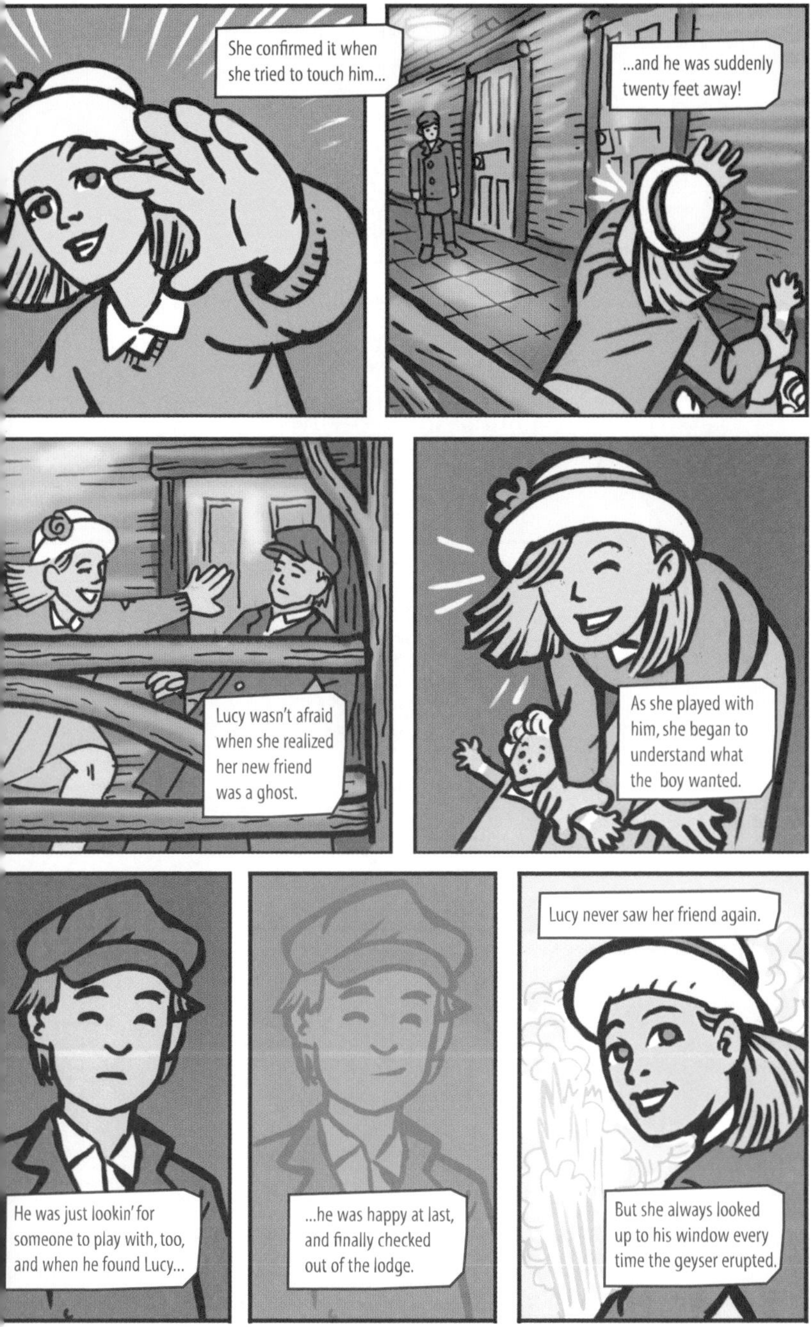
She confirmed it when she tried to touch him...
...and he was suddenly twenty feet away!
Lucy wasn't afraid when she realized her new friend was a ghost.
As she played with him, she began to understand what the boy wanted.
He was just lookin' for someone to play with, too, and when he found Lucy...
...he was happy at last, and finally checked out of the lodge.
Lucy never saw her friend again.
But she always looked up to his window every time the geyser erupted.

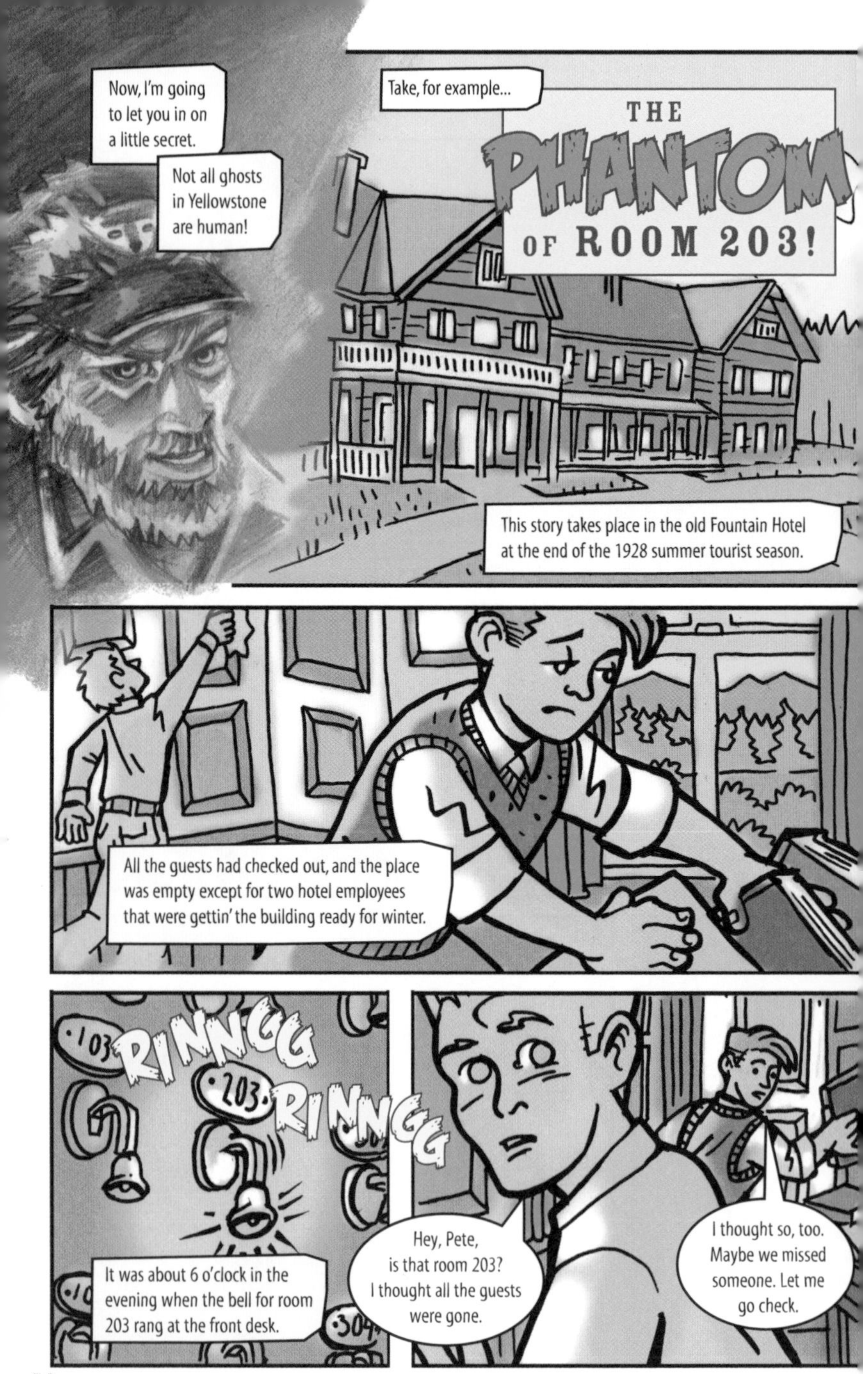
Now, I'm going to let you in on a little secret.
Not all ghosts in Yellowstone are human!
Take, for example...
THE PHANTOM OF ROOM 203!
This story takes place in the old Fountain Hotel at the end of the 1928 summer tourist season.
All the guests had checked out, and the place was empty except for two hotel employees that were gettin' the building ready for winter.
103
RINNGG
203
RINNGG
It was about 6 o'clock in the evening when the bell for room 203 rang at the front desk.
304
Hey, Pete, is that room 203? I thought all the guests were gone.
I thought so, too. Maybe we missed someone. Let me go check.

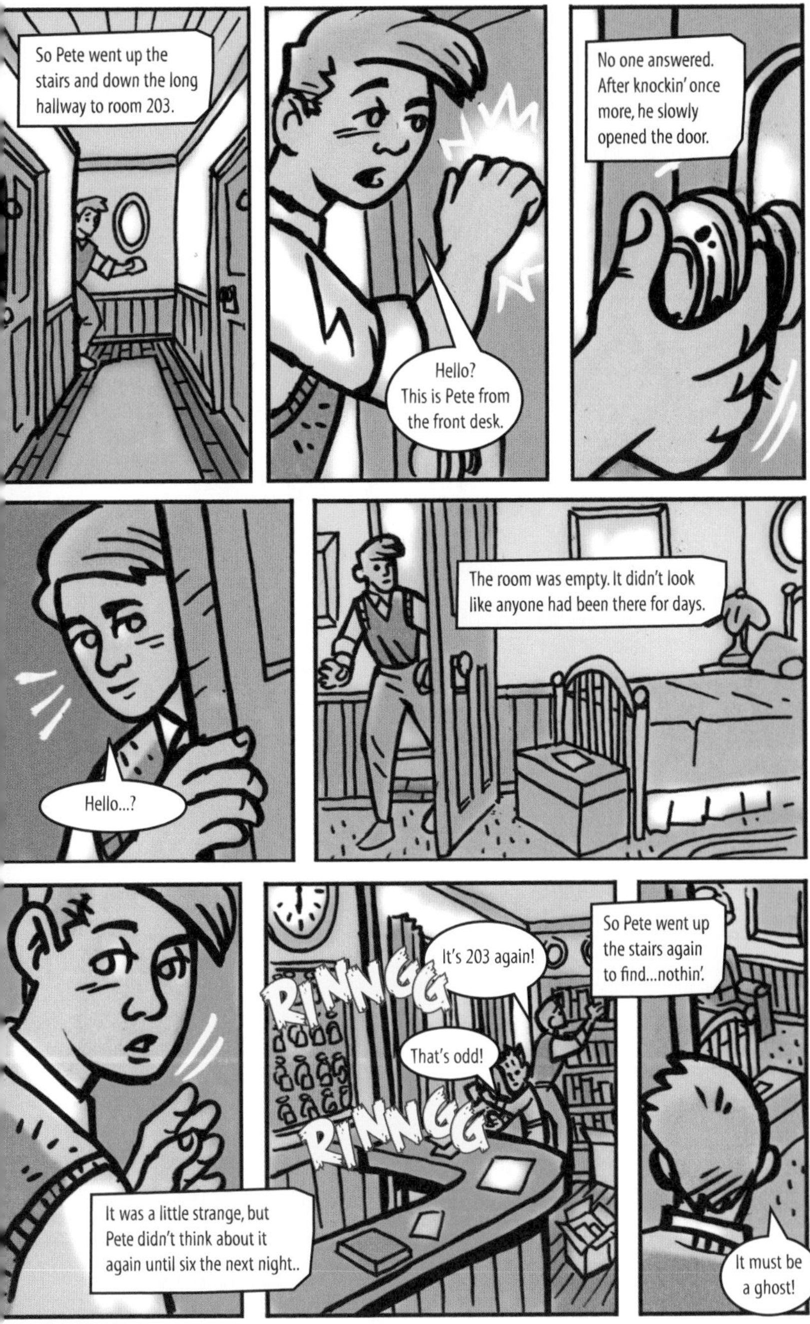
So Pete went up the stairs and down the long hallway to room 203.
Hello? This is Pete from the front desk.
No one answered. After knockin' once more, he slowly opened the door.
Hello...?
The room was empty. It didn't look like anyone had been there for days.
It was a little strange, but Pete didn't think about it again until six the next night..
RINNGG
It's 203 again!
That's odd!
RINNGG
So Pete went up the stairs again to find...nothin'.
It must be a ghost!

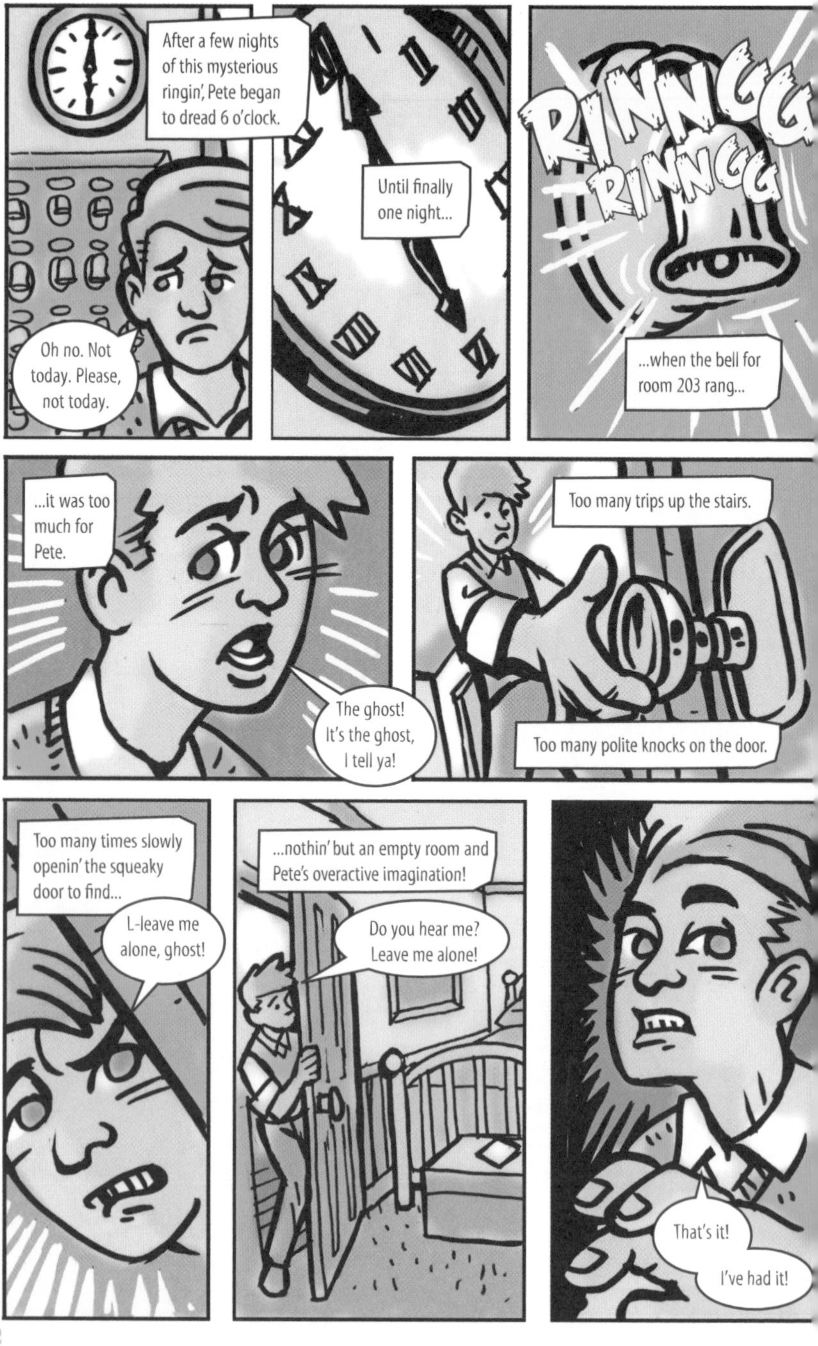
After a few nights of this mysterious ringin', Pete began to dread 6 o'clock.
Oh no. Not today. Please, not today.
Until finally one night...
RINNGG RINNGG
...when the bell for room 203 rang...
...it was too much for Pete.
The ghost! It's the ghost, I tell ya!
Too many trips up the stairs.
Too many polite knocks on the door.
Too many times slowly openin' the squeaky door to find...
L-leave me alone, ghost!
...nothin' but an empty room and Pete's overactive imagination!
Do you hear me? Leave me alone!
That's it!
I've had it!

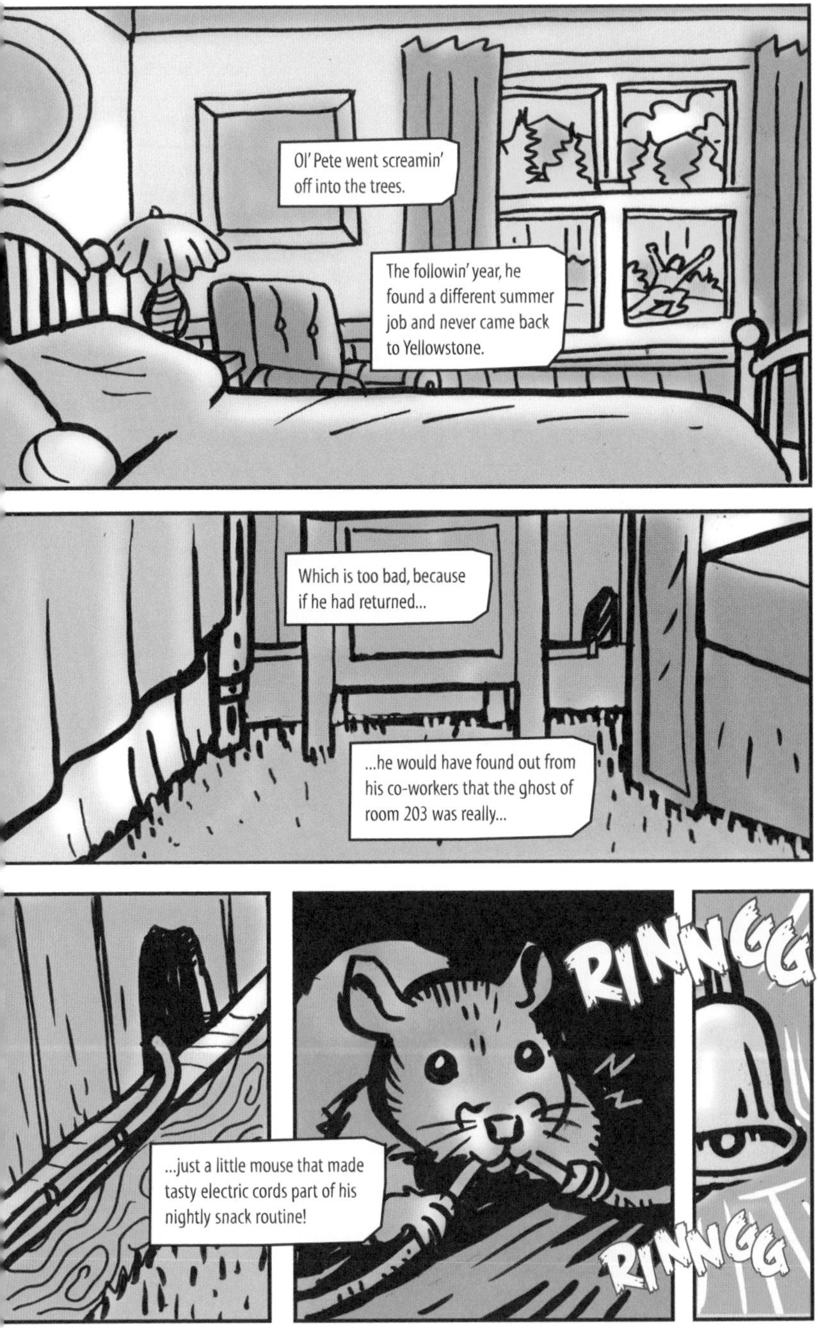
Ol' Pete went screamin' off into the trees.
The followin' year, he found a different summer job and never came back to Yellowstone.
Which is too bad, because if he had returned...
...he would have found out from his co-workers that the ghost of room 203 was really...
...just a little mouse that made tasty electric cords part of his nightly snack routine!
RINNGG
RINNGG

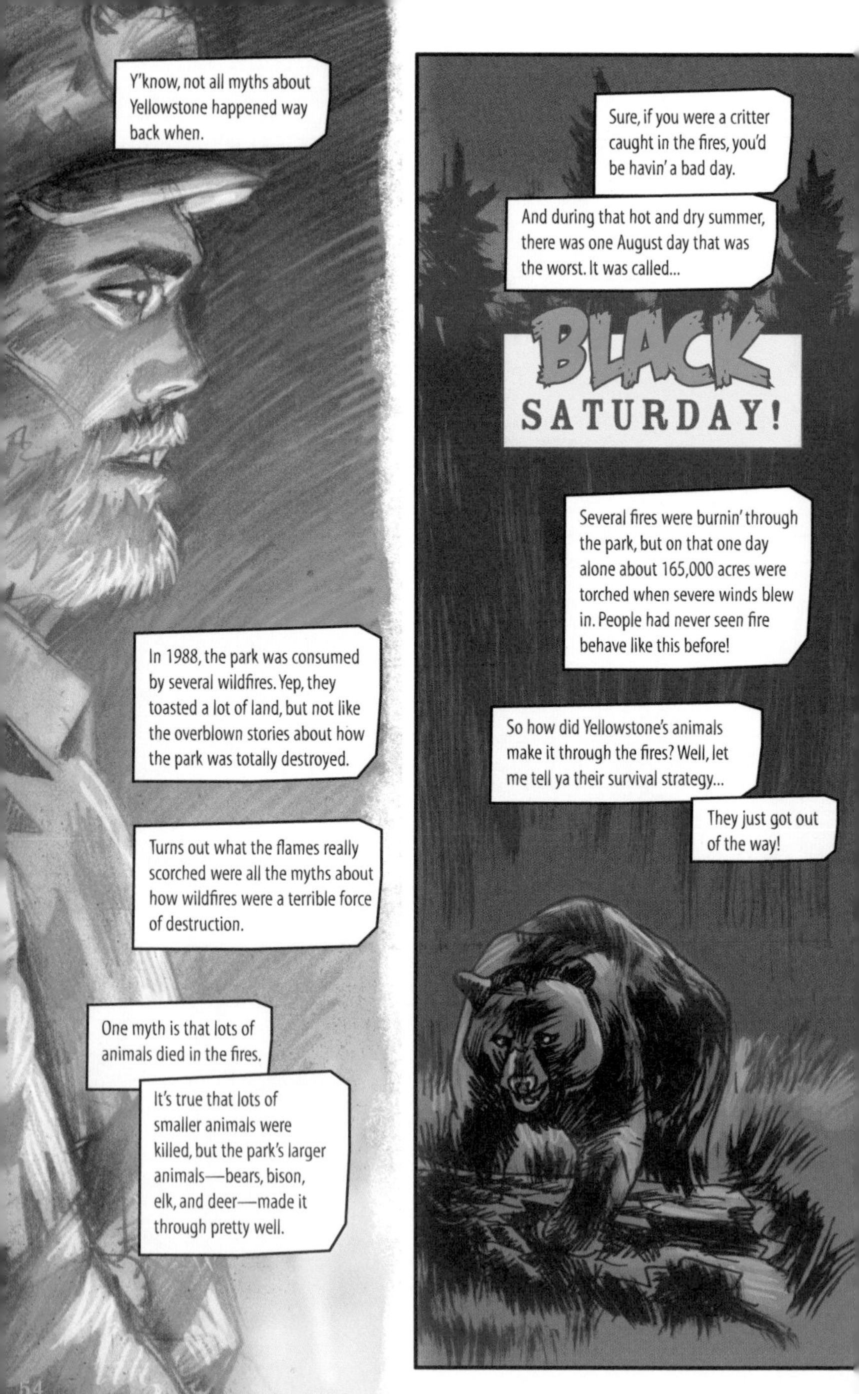

Y'know, not all myths about Yellowstone happened way back when.
In 1988, the park was consumed by several wildfires. Yep, they toasted a lot of land, but not like the overblown stories about how the park was totally destroyed.
Turns out what the flames really scorched were all the myths about how wildfires were a terrible force of destruction.
One myth is that lots of animals died in the fires.
It's true that lots of smaller animals were killed, but the park's larger animals—bears, bison, elk, and deer—made it through pretty well.
Sure, if you were a critter caught in the fires, you'd be havin' a bad day.
And during that hot and dry summer, there was one August day that was the worst. It was called...
BLACK SATURDAY!
Several fires were burnin' through the park, but on that one day alone about 165,000 acres were torched when severe winds blew in. People had never seen fire behave like this before!
So how did Yellowstone's animals make it through the fires? Well, let me tell ya their survival strategy...
They just got out of the way!

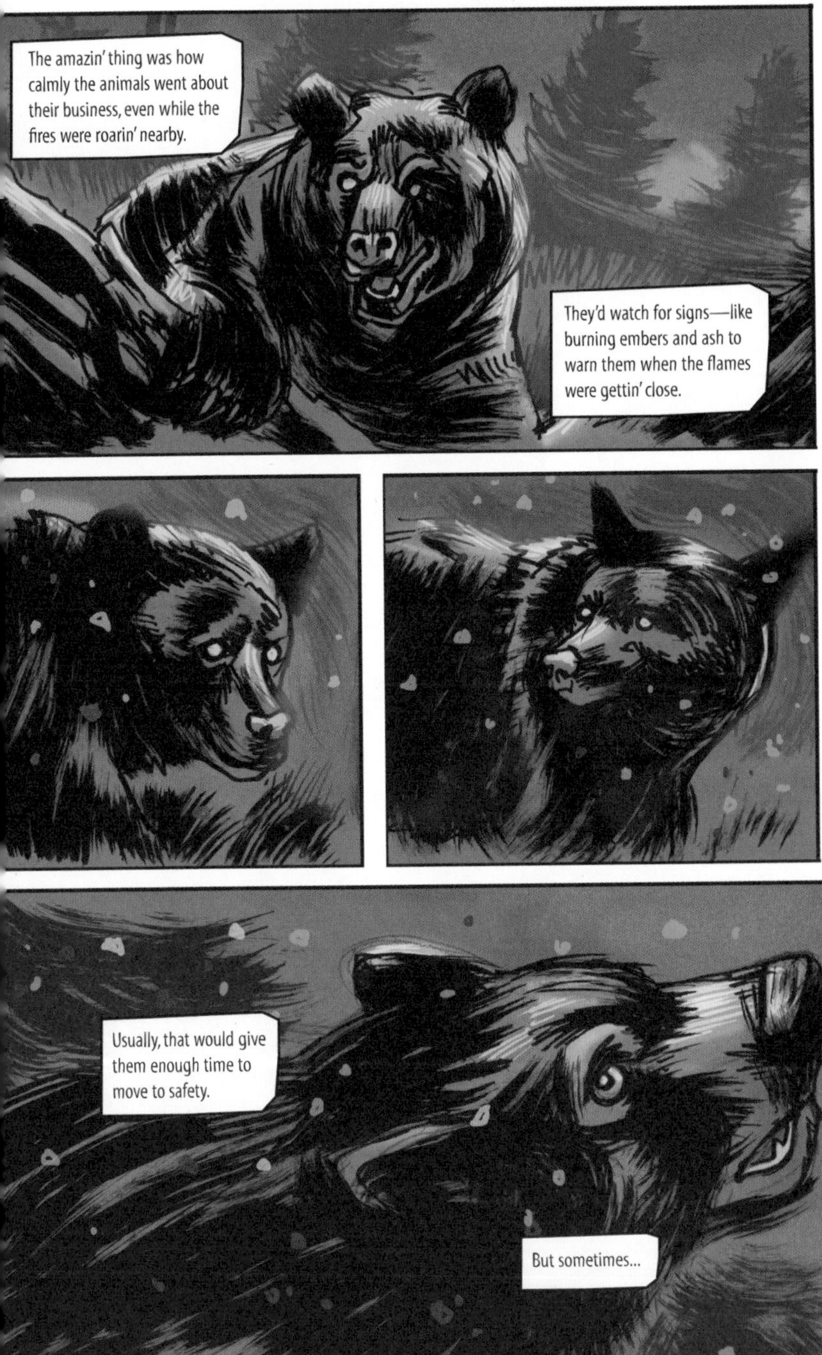
The amazin' thing was how calmly the animals went about their business, even while the fires were roarin' nearby.
They'd watch for signs—like burning embers and ash to warn them when the flames were gettin' close.
Usually, that would give them enough time to move to safety.
But sometimes...

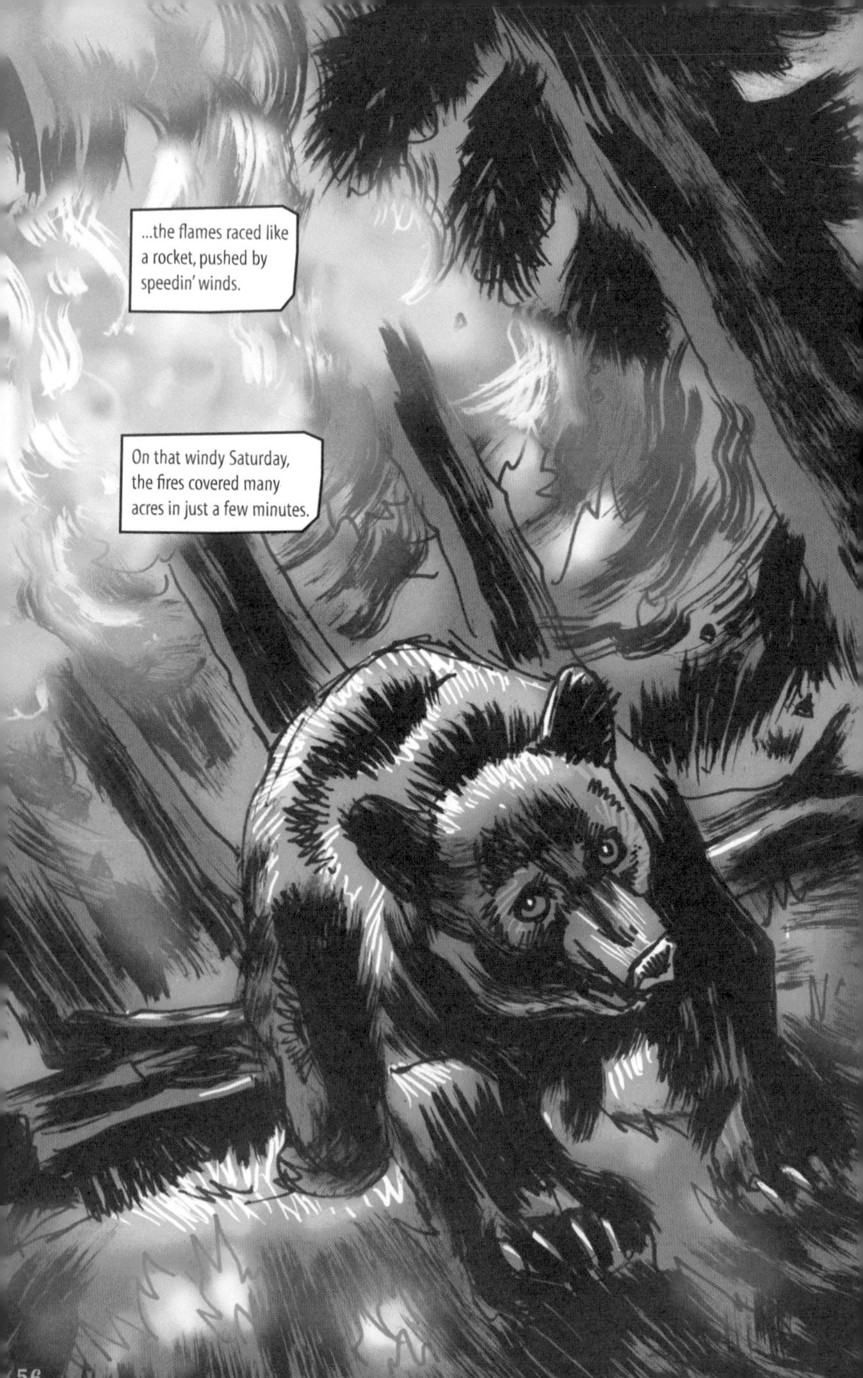
...the flames raced like a rocket, pushed by speedin' winds.
On that windy Saturday, the fires covered many acres in just a few minutes.

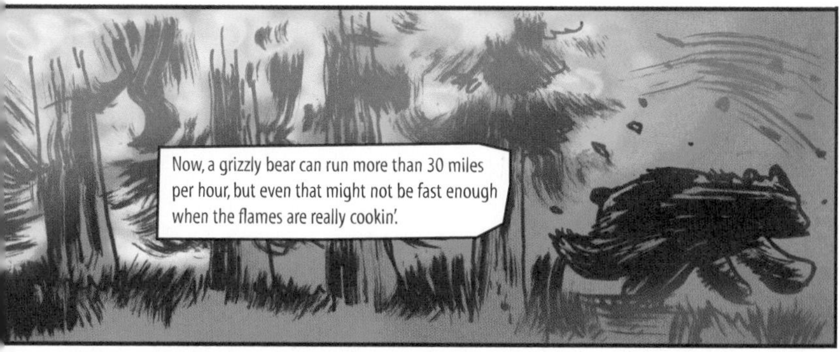
Now, a grizzly bear can run more than 30 miles per hour, but even that might not be fast enough when the flames are really cookin'.

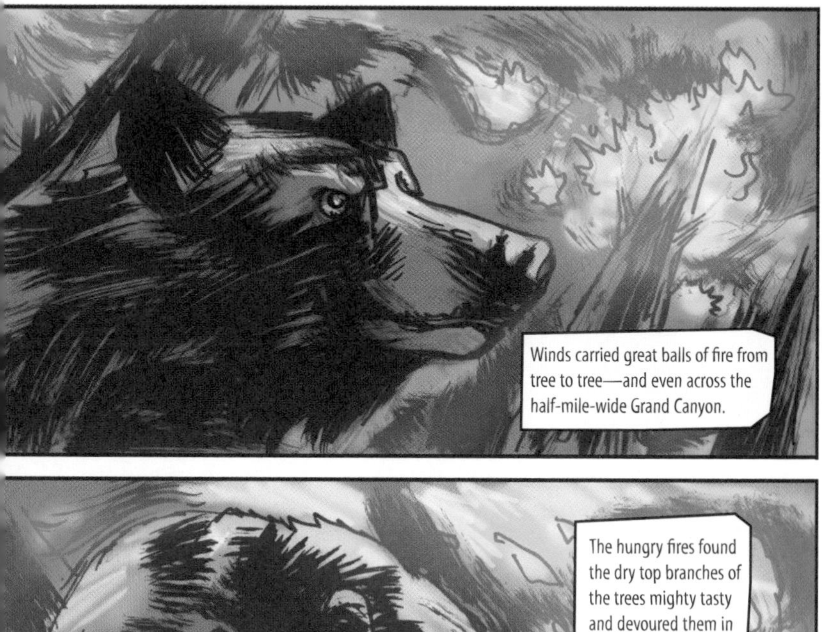
Winds carried great balls of fire from tree to tree—and even across the half-mile-wide Grand Canyon.

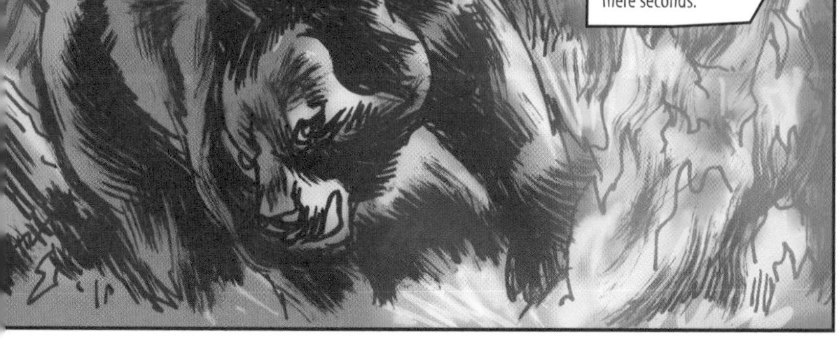
The hungry fires found the dry top branches of the trees mighty tasty and devoured them in mere seconds.

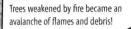

Trees weakened by fire became an avalanche of flames and debris!

Finally, September snowfall began to put out the fires. In the end, more than 790,000 acres—that's 36% of the park—had been blackened.

Parts of the once-lush landscape were now grey and barren, like the surface of the moon.

And that ignited another round of myths...

Like: Giant fires aren't natural and have never happened before...

Or: The charred land will never be green again...

And my favorite: No visitors or animals will ever want to come back.

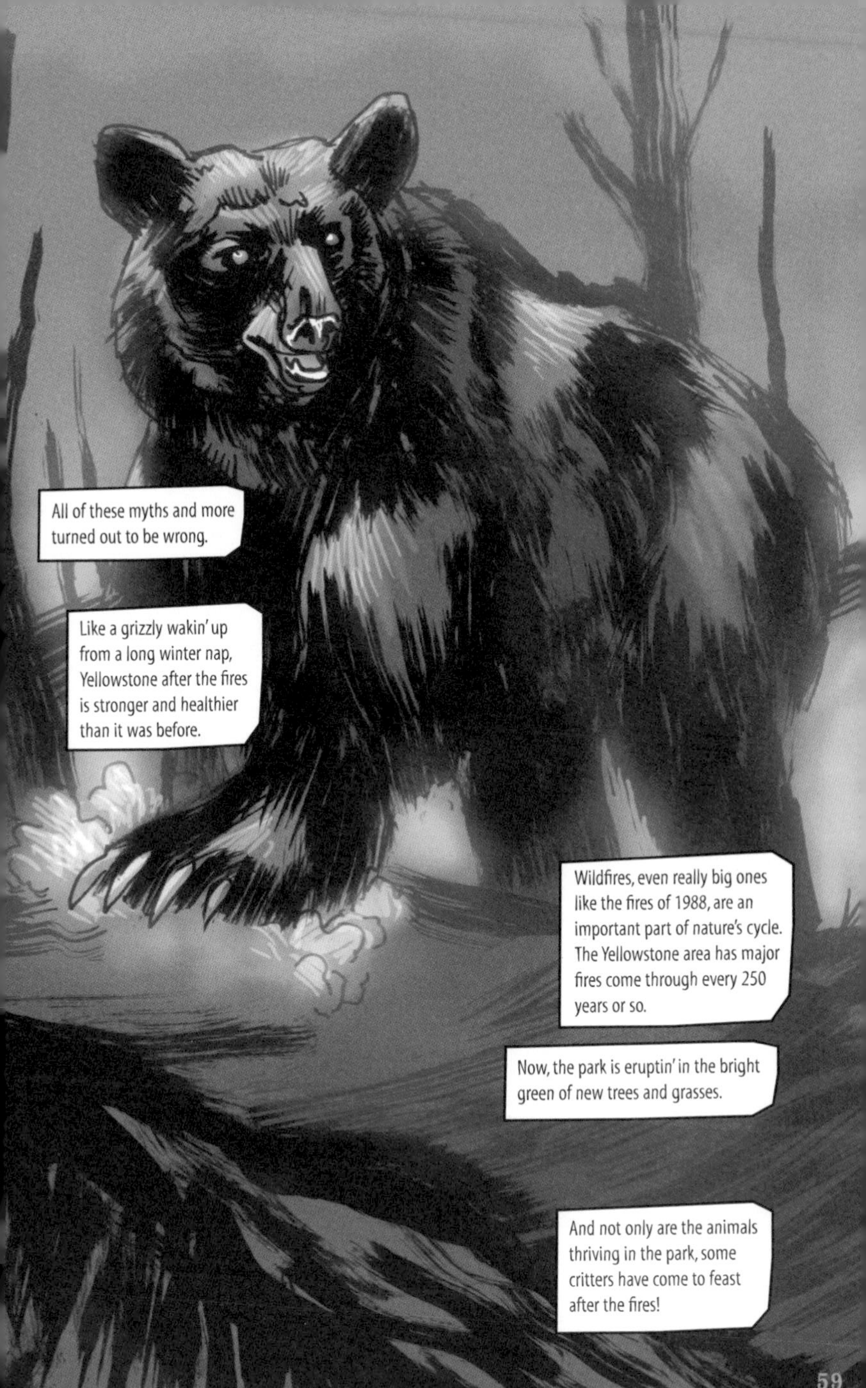
All of these myths and more turned out to be wrong.
Like a grizzly wakin' up from a long winter nap, Yellowstone after the fires is stronger and healthier than it was before.
Wildfires, even really big ones like the fires of 1988, are an important part of nature's cycle. The Yellowstone area has major fires come through every 250 years or so.
Now, the park is eruptin' in the bright green of new trees and grasses.
And not only are the animals thriving in the park, some critters have come to feast after the fires!

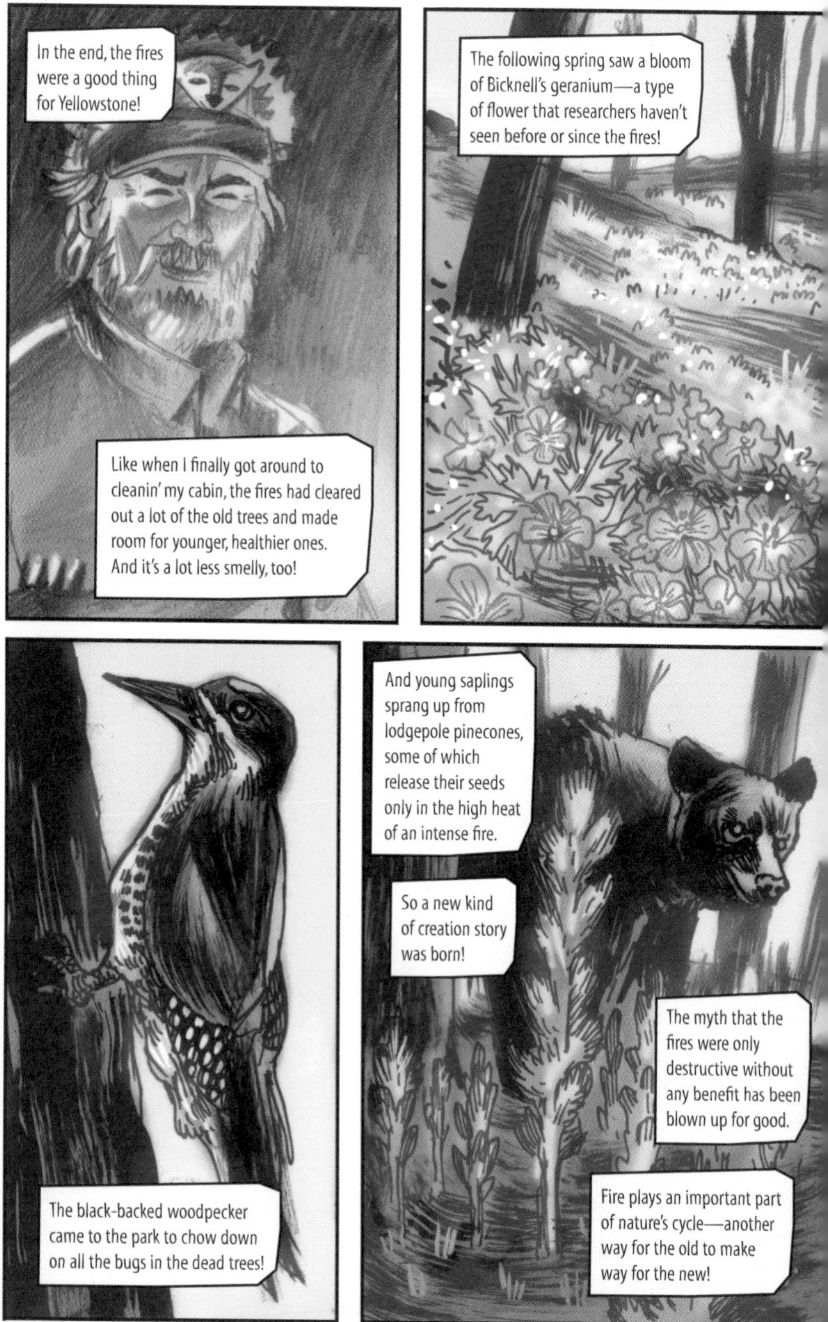
In the end, the fires were a good thing for Yellowstone!
Like when I finally got around to cleanin' my cabin, the fires had cleared out a lot of the old trees and made room for younger, healthier ones. And it's a lot less smelly, too!
The following spring saw a bloom of Bicknell's geranium—a type of flower that researchers haven't seen before or since the fires!
The black-backed woodpecker came to the park to chow down on all the bugs in the dead trees!
And young saplings sprang up from lodgepole pinecones, some of which release their seeds only in the high heat of an intense fire.
So a new kind of creation story was born!
The myth that the fires were only destructive without any benefit has been blown up for good.
Fire plays an important part of nature's cycle—another way for the old to make way for the new!

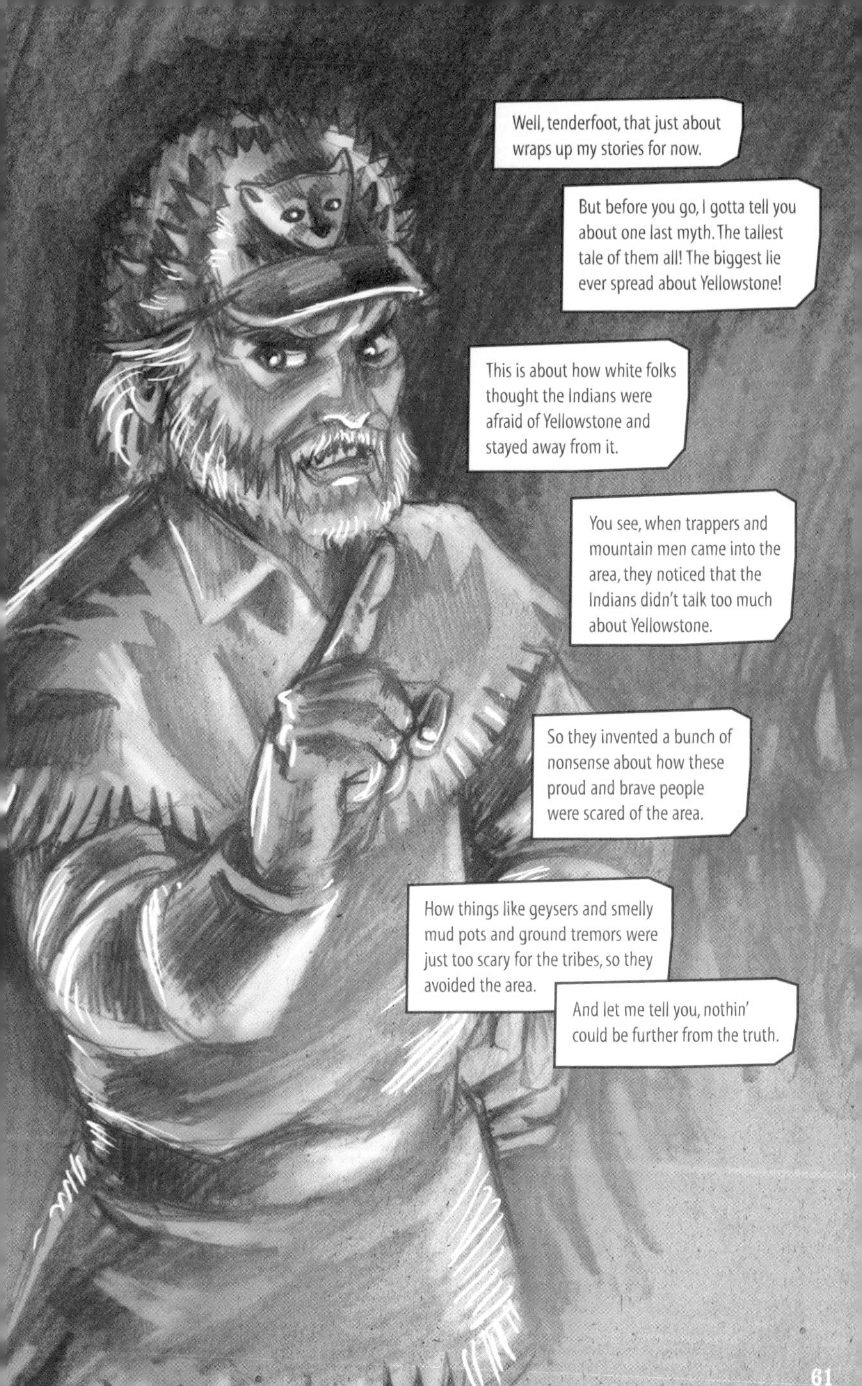
Well, tenderfoot, that just about wraps up my stories for now.
But before you go, I gotta tell you about one last myth. The tallest tale of them all! The biggest lie ever spread about Yellowstone!
This is about how white folks thought the Indians were afraid of Yellowstone and stayed away from it.
You see, when trappers and mountain men came into the area, they noticed that the Indians didn't talk too much about Yellowstone.
So they invented a bunch of nonsense about how these proud and brave people were scared of the area.
How things like geysers and smelly mud pots and ground tremors were just too scary for the tribes, so they avoided the area.
And let me tell you, nothin' could be further from the truth.

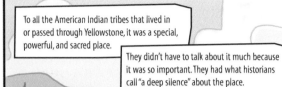

To all the American Indian tribes that lived in or passed through Yellowstone, it was a special, powerful, and sacred place.

They didn't have to talk about it much because it was so important. They had what historians call "a deep silence" about the place.

But if you ask me, that "deep silence" is more than the absence of words.

It's that feelin' you get when you are here. That feelin' of being part of somethin' big. Somethin' that's been here a long time.

For the Indians, being in Yellowstone meant being close to their gods and closer to the events that created the world.

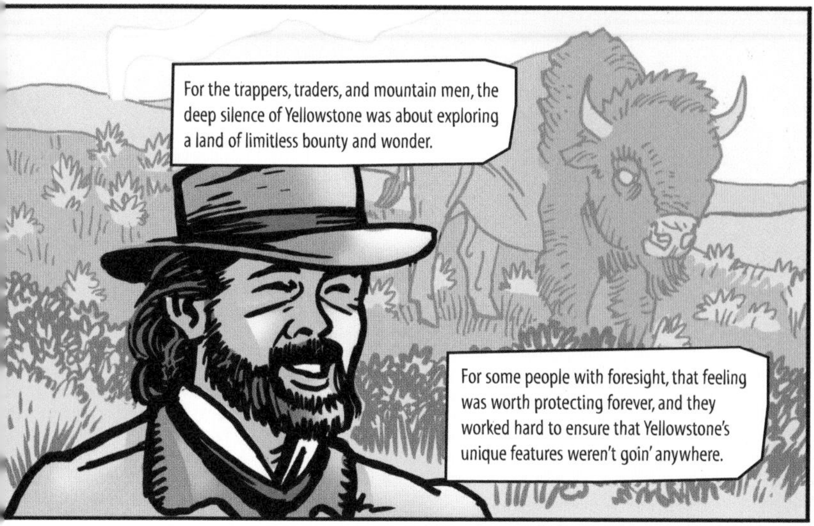
For the trappers, traders, and mountain men, the deep silence of Yellowstone was about exploring a land of limitless bounty and wonder.
For some people with foresight, that feeling was worth protecting forever, and they worked hard to ensure that Yellowstone's unique features weren't goin' anywhere.

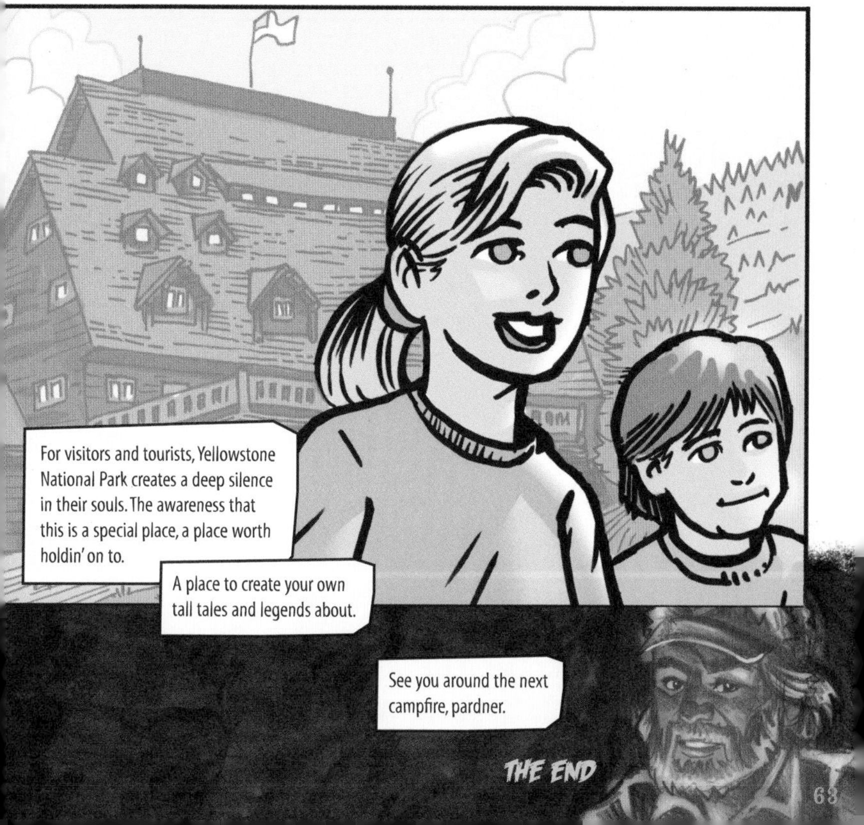
For visitors and tourists, Yellowstone National Park creates a deep silence in their souls. The awareness that this is a special place, a place worth holdin' on to.
A place to create your own tall tales and legends about.
See you around the next campfire, pardner.
THE END

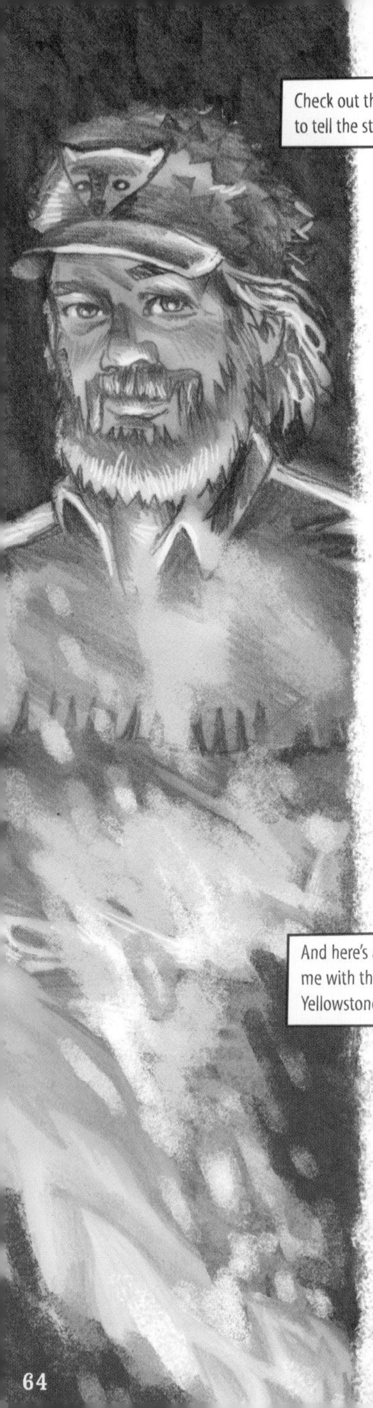

Check out this list of all the references I used to tell the stories you read in this here book!

Restoring a Presence: American Indians and Yellowstone National Park by Peter Nabokov, University of Oklahoma Press, 2004

A Woman Tenderfoot by Grace Gallatin Seton-Thompson, Doubleday, Page & Co., 1900

Myth and History in the Creation of Yellowstone National Park by Paul Schullery, University of Nebraska Press, 2003

Indians in Yellowstone National Park by Joel C. Janetski, University of Utah Press, 2002

The Yellowstone Story: A History of Our First National Park by Aubrey L. Haines, Yellowstone Association for Natural Science, History & Education, 1977, 1996

Yellowstone: 125 Years of America's Best Idea by Michael Milstein, Billings Gazette, 1996

The Yellowstone Park Fire of 1988 by Melanie Ann Apel, Rosen Pub. Group, Inc., 2004

Fire in the Forest: A Cycle of Growth and Renewal by Laurence P. Pringle, Atheneum Books for Young Readers, 1995

Yellowstone on Fire! by Robert Ekey, Billings Gazette, 1989

Yellowstone's Rebirth by Fire: Rising from the Ashes of the 1988 Wildfires by Karen Reinhart, Farcountry Press, 2008

Yellowstone Ghost Stories by Shellie Herzog Larios, Riverbend Publishing, 2006

"Native Americans, the Earliest Interpreters: What is Known About Their Legends and Stories of Yellowstone National Park and the Complexities of Interpreting Them" by Lee H. Whittlesey, The George Wright Society, 2005, www.georgewright.org/01yp_whittlesey.pdf

Sly Mouse Ghost of Park Hotel, The Davenport Iowa Democrat and Leader, June 13, 1928

"Yellowstone: A Study in Vital Role of Wildfires," by Julie Cart, LA Times, July 8, 2002, http://articles.latimes.com/2002/jul/08/nation/na-yellow8

And here's a list of some mighty nice people that helped me with this book! I give them a "thank you" deeper than Yellowstone Lake and taller than Eagle Peak.

A big geyser of thanks to Jessica Solberg, who made the project happen and was super-patient while it took forever to get it done!

Thanks to Tobin and Caroline Patterson for exploring the book early in its history.

Thanks to Karen Reinhart for keeping me from getting burned on the details.

Thanks to everyone at Farcountry — Kathy, Shirley, Theresa, Kelli, and Eric — for providing a great environment for work.

And thanks to Kathy, Lucy, and Thomas for all the trips to the park and bearing with all my late nights around the campfire!